SCIENCE ON THE INTERNET

A RESOURCE FOR K-12 TEACHERS

Second Edition

Jazlin V. Ebenezer
Wayne State University

Eddy Lau
University of Manitoba

Merrill
Prentice Hall

Upper Saddle River, New Jersey
Columbus, Ohio

Library of Congress Cataloging-in-Publication Data

Ebenezer, Jazlin V.
  Science on the Internet : a resource for K-12 teachers / by Jazlin V. Ebenezer, Eddy
Lau.—2nd ed.
    p. cm.
  Includes bibliographical references.
  ISBN 0-13-060795-9 (pbk.)
    1. Science—Study and teaching—Computer network resources.   2. Internet in
    education.
  I. Lau, Eddy.   II. Title.

LB1585 .E189 2003
507'.1—dc21

                                                                2002075378

Vice President and Publisher: Jeffery W. Johnston
Editor: Linda Ashe Montgomery
Production Editor: Mary M. Irvin
Design Coordinator: Diane C. Lorenzo
Text Design and Production Coordination: Clarinda Publication Services
Cover Designer: Heather Miller
Cover Art: Index Stock
Production Manager: Susan Hannahs
Director of Marketing: Ann Castel Davis
Marketing Manager: Darcy Betts
Marketing Services Manager: Tyra Cooper

This book was set in Minion by The Clarinda Company, and was printed and bound
by R. R. Donnelley & Sons Company. The cover was printed by Phoenix Color Corp.

Pearson Education Ltd.
Pearson Education Australia Pty. Limited.
Pearson Education Singapore Pte. Ltd.
Pearson Education North Asia Ltd.
Pearson Education Canada, Ltd.
Pearson Educación de Mexico, S.A. de C.V.
Pearson Education—Japan, *Tokyo*
Pearson Education Malaysia Pte. Ltd.
Pearson Education, *Upper Saddle River, New Jersey*

10 9 8 7 6 5 4 3 2
ISBN 0-13-060795-9

For our mentor, colleague, and friend,
Dexter Harvey

For my loving son and Eddy's best friend,
Sudesh Ebenezer

PREFACE

Science on the Internet is in part a collection of science education Web sites useful for college students preparing to teach science; science teacher educators; and teachers in elementary, middle, and secondary classrooms. Science content-based Web sites as well as Web sites pertaining to curricular topics, trends, and issues in science education are included. This collection also offers time-tested sites: government-sponsored, secure companies that we hope will be around for years to come. All of the sites have been reviewed carefully to ensure that content is useful and up to date.

Chapter 1 describes briefly what the Internet is and how to use it. We have also provided a list of Internet tutorial sites that will teach how to surf the Net. We also show a way of narrowing Internet searches in science. This chapter, therefore, helps teachers to become Internet literate.

Chapter 2 presents a philosophy of science teaching for the 21st century in elementary, middle, and secondary schools. With the help of several screen captures from established Internet resources, we discuss how the Internet can be used in the context of science education. This chapter includes case studies of teachers at various levels (university, secondary, and elementary) using the Internet in their classrooms. It also suggests ways of integrating the Internet into science teaching. In particular, the sections on virtual field trips, conducting research, and joint classroom projects are valuable for science teachers and their students.

Chapter 3 is the heart of the resource guide. It contains a wealth of resources that every science teacher will find useful. We have grouped each of the sites into categories that are similar to the topics outlined in the "science content standards" (National Research Council, 1996). The topical outline is as follows:

- Earth and Space Science
- Life Science
- Physical Science
- General Science
- Elementary Science
- Secondary Science
- K-12 Science

- Science, Technology, and Society Connections
- Integrating Science and Other Curricular Areas

Each of the suggested sites is annotated to provide content and insights about a particular homepage. Each of the entries in Chapter 3 is based on the following scale:

R   Rating (* = Average, ** = Very Good)

GL   Grade Level

TCK   Teacher Content Knowledge

RR   Research Reports

STS   Science Technology and Society

IL   Inquiry Lessons

RTD   Real Time Data

Chapter 4 identifies many sites that provide current ideas concerning conceptual change in scientific thinking. In addition, it lists sites that lead to important instructional information, including links to science assessment, journal writing, girls and science, multicultural science education, informal learning, and professional science organizations.

A good assignment for prospective teachers is to review at least 10 sites from this book in an annotated WWW bibliography format, then to share those comments with all class members.

ACKNOWLEDGMENTS

We kindly remember the technical assistance that Scott Wellman, Faculty of Education at the University of Manitoba, has continuously provided us. We acknowledge Dr. Joel Bass, Sam Houston State University, for providing us with materials on Real Time Data. We also thank all of our reviewers for their helpful suggestions: Joel Bass, Sam Houston State University; John R. Cannon, University of Nevada-Reno; Joseph Peters, University of West Florida; Martha Nabors, College of Charleston; Lita Duncan Burnett, Cumberland University; Richard Pontius, University of Missouri–St. Louis; Donna T. Powers, Western Illinois University; Thomas Goodkind, University of Connecticut; Tony L. Talbert, Sam Houston State University; Donna Merkley, Iowa State University; Harold Nelson, Minot State University; and Anna Bolling, California State University–Stanislaus. We have attempted to incorporate their useful comments into this book.

Jazlin V. Ebenezer, Ed.D.
Eddy Lau, B.Sc.

CONTENTS

Note: Every effort has been made to provide accurate and current Internet information in this book. However, the Internet and information posted on it are constantly changing, so it is inevitable that some of the Internet addresses in this textbook will change.

1

SURFING THE NETSCAPE BROWSER

- The Internet
- Surfing the Internet
- Sites for Internet Guides and Tutorials
- Narrowing Searches for Net-Worthy Sites

THE INTERNET

The Internet is a huge network of interconnected computer networks linking the whole world (see Figure 1–1). For example, the computers in a college of education can be linked to form a network of computers. This is what is known as a LAN (local area network). This single network of computers is connected to other colleges in the same university, and the university computer network is then connected to a series of networks in other universities, school networks, commercial and business networks, government networks, industry networks, and every other network in the world, transcending geographical barriers. All of the computer networks have multilevel connections with telephone, radio, and satellite. Intercontinental telephone and fiber-optic connection lines running beneath the ocean floor link all the continents.

Figure 1-1   The Internet

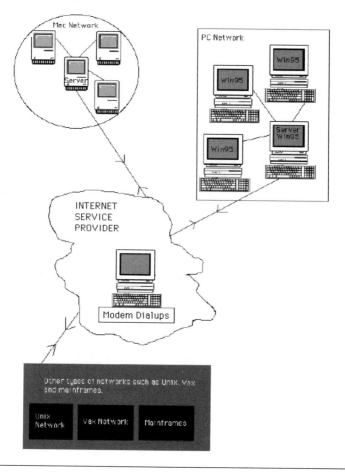

The Internet consists of information servers that include Web sites. An increasing number of Web sites are added each day to the Internet, thus making it more difficult to find relevant information. The emergence of search engines and search directories has harnessed the overflow of Web sites. With search engines and definitive subject and topic searches, information and resources on the Internet can be quickly located and extracted. The Internet browser (e.g., Microsoft Internet Explorer and Netscape) provides a "graphic interface to the Internet and the World Wide Web allowing for exploration of information via hot buttons which link to further resources" (Morris, 1996). This shows you how to surf the Internet, connect to numerous sites, and communicate as well as collaborate.

What Is an Internet Address?

Each computer in the Internet is tagged or personalized with a set of numbers or letters, which is known as the IP (Internet Protocol) address. The Internet Protocol address enables you to search, locate, reach, and connect to a specific computer that provides the information for which you are looking. To find a Web site in the Internet, a set of syntax or procedures must be followed and this syntax connects to the computer that holds the particular information.

The Internet Web site address is called a URL, which stands for Uniform Resource Locator. An example of a URL for a Web site is:

http://www.exploratorium.edu/sport/index.html

The standard format for a URL is:

protocol://host.domain[:port][/path][filename] in which

- the *protocol* is http (Hypertext Transport Protocol) for the http information server
- *host.domain* stands for www.exploratorium.edu
- *path* represents / sport
- *filename* stands for index.html

This standard format or syntax allows the browser client software to recognize and to make the appropriate connections to the location of the Web sites. This is somewhat similar to telephone or mail area codes.

Information Servers

On the Internet there are different types of information services: *http, gopher, telnet,* and *ftp*. These services present information in different layouts and styles. *Http* features text, sound, graphics, and movie capabilities. In contrast, *gopher* and *telnet* information services are only text based.

Ftp (File Transfer Protocol), as the name indicates, is a protocol for transferring files from one computer to another. But all services use the same standard URL format. (See the section "What is an Internet Address?") If you need to change from one information server to another—for example, from the *http* information service to a *telnet* information service—change your protocol as follows:

from **http://www. exploratorium.edu/sport/index.html**
to **telnet://mira.cc.umanitoba.ca/**

SURFING THE INTERNET

How to Connect to a Web Site With a URL Address

1. Type the URL address in the "Go to" Box (sometimes referred to as the Location Box or Netsite Box) in the Netscape Browser.

2. Press return. You will be connected to the site. (See Figure 1–1.)

Steps to Search a Web Site of Your Choice

1. Click on the Net Search button on the Netscape Browser. You will see several search engines:
   - Excite
   - Infoseek
   - Lycos
   - Altavista
   - Magellan
   - Webcrawler
2. Select one of the search engines by clicking on it. You will see a rectangular box.
3. Click inside the box so that your cursor is in the box.
4. Type the subject or topic of your search in the rectangular box.

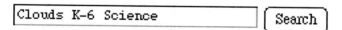

5. Click on the Search button as shown. You will now see a listing of "hits" of the topic or subject.
6. Click on the blue hypertext, also underlined in blue.

   Note: The links to the search engine are available in our support program.

Figure 1-2 Netscape

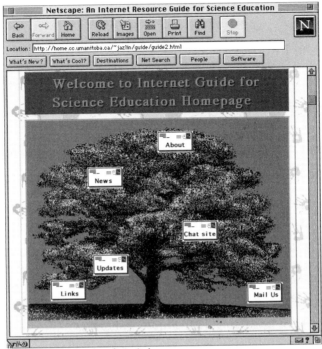

Source: Dr. Jazlin Ebenezer, University of Manitoba.

URL Address for Search Engine

Since the Net Search button (see Figure 1–2) is a link to all of the search engine sites, proper connections will not be made if the Net search server goes down. Therefore, we have provided you with the URL for each of the main search engines in the Internet (see Table 1–1).

Table 1-1

Search Engine	Uniform Resource Locator (URL)
1. Google	http://www.google.com
2. AlltheWeb	http://www.alltheweb.com/
3. Metacrawler	http://www.metacrawler.com
4. Excite	http://www.excite.com
5. Yahoo	http://www.yahoo.com
6. Hotbot	http://www.hotbot.com

Choose a search engine from Table 1–1 and type the corresponding address in the Location Box in the Netscape Browser. Then repeat steps 2 through 6 described under "Steps to Search a Web Site of Your Choice."

Zones on the Internet

The URL consists of zones (see *com* and *ca* in the URL below) that represent the domain or the name of the host computer.

http://www.investorsgroup.*com*
http://www.umanitoba.*ca*

The term *com, edu,* or *ca* in the domain of the URL represents an organization or country.

Downloading Information From the Internet Onto Local Hard Drives

You can actually download resources from any of the information servers on the Internet to your hard drive or to a computer disk. This function is useful to minimize on-line costs in the Internet and to incorporate resources into your personal work.

Steps for Downloading Using a Macintosh Computer

1. Click with your mouse on the hypertext you want and hold. (Note: On the PC Windows 2000 Operating Systems, the process is the same, but you have to click on the right button of your mouse and hold.)
   You will see a menu of options such as "save image as," "save link as," and "copy picture."
2. Select an option provided.
   You will see a box requesting you to specify where to put the downloaded file.
3. Click on the Save button to save either on the hard drive or on your personal disk.

SITES FOR INTERNET GUIDES AND TUTORIALS

There are guides and tutorials on the Internet that will assist you in surfing the Internet. Please go through the following URLs of Web sites if you want to learn more about surfing the Internet. To inform you as to what sorts of materials are available in the tutorial guides, we have included the table of contents for the first two electronic books listed.

The Complete Internet Guide and Web Tutorial
http://www.microsoft.com/insider/internet/

A virtual tour of the World Wide Web. Provides beginners with tutorials and guides. Listed below is the table of contents that is available on this site:

- Introduction
- Browser Basics I
- Browser Basics II
- Internet Explorer 5, I
- Internet Explorer 5, II
- Online Search Tips
- Advanced Search Tips
- Getting Online I
- Getting Online II
- All About E-mail
- Find it Online, I
- Find it Online, II
- Banking & Investing
- Internet Security I
- Internet Security II
- Creating a Web Site I
- Creating a Web Site II
- Multimedia on the Web
- History of the Internet

The RoadMap to the Internet
http://www.webreference.com/roadmap/

Covers the practical aspects of using the Internet. It is excellent for beginners. Listed below is the table of contents available on this site:

WEEK 1

lesson description

INTRO	ROADMAP96 INTRODUCTION
MAP01	WELCOME
MAP02	LISTSERV FILE SERVER COMMANDS

WEEK 2

lesson description

MAP03	LEVELS OF INTERNET CONNECTIVITY
MAP04	E-MAIL
MAP05	LISTSERVS
MAP06	OTHER MAIL SERVERS
MAP07	NETIQUETTE

WEEK 3

lesson description

MAP08	USENET
MAP09	SPAMMING AND URBAN LEGENDS
MAP10	INTERNET SECURITY
MAP11	TELNET (PART ONE)
MAP12	TELNET (PART TWO)

WEEK 4

lesson description

MAP13	FTP (PART ONE)
MAP14	FTP (PART TWO)
MAP15	FTPMAIL
MAP16	FTP FILE COMPRESSION
MAP17	ARCHIE
MAP17B	FTP SITES

WEEK 5

lesson description

MAP18	GOPHER (PART ONE)
MAP19	GOPHER (PART TWO)
MAP20	BOOKMARKS AND BOOKLISTS
MAP21	VERONICA
MAP22	GOPHERMAIL

WEEK 6

lesson description

MAP23	WWW (PART ONE)
MAP24	WWW (PART TWO)
MAP25	ADDRESS SEARCHES AND FINGER
NEAT	MAP-EXTRA: NEAT STUFF TO CHECK OUT
ADVERT	ADVERTISING ON THE INTERNET
MAP26	IRC/MUDs/MOOs AND OTHER "TALKERS"
SMITH	GUEST LECTURER-RICHARD SMITH
MAP27	THE FUTURE . . .

Ask Dr. Internet
http://www.promo.net/drnet/

Extensive archive provides answers to common questions about the Web. Search for posting stories, or submit your own question.

Internet Web Text (Index)
http://www.december.com/web/text/index.html

Has a collection of most of the guides and tutorials that are available on the Internet.

Internet Guides, Tutorials, and Training Information
http://www.loc.gov/loc/guides/

Explore and download some of the documents that this library of Internet guides and tutorials offers in this Web site. Make sure you download the latest documents to get up-to-date information.

Polaris Internet Tour
http://www.provide.net/~bfield/polaris/tour0000.htm

An on-line tour of the Internet provides essential basics of how to use the Internet that make surfing easy for the beginner. It also includes topics such as ISDN, FTP, WWW, and USENET.

Internet Starter Kit
http://www.tidbits.com/iskm/iskw2html/toc.html

Connects to the latest Windows editions of the classic Internet guide that links to various topics about the Internet.

Internet 101
http://www2.famvid.com/i101/

Provides the basics on using the Net. Includes tips on searching, using e-mail, newsgroups, and chatrooms.

Jay Barker's Online Connection
http://www.barkers.org/online/

Compares major U.S. Internet service providers based on the connection's speed, price, software, features, and support.

SafeKids
http://www.safekids.com/

Provides step-by-step on-line tutorials and instructions on how children can use the Internet safely. Resources and information are available for both parents and children.

Learning Online
http://www.ualberta.ca/~maldridg/tutor/Tutorials.html

Provides a directory of Web-based tutorials for using the Internet, Web tools, Ethernet, and programming languages such as Java.

Life on the Internet
http://www.screen.com/start/welcome.html

This beginners' guide gives over 300 links as well as tips on using the browsers.

Mac Internet Connect Guide
http://www.i-55.com/mac2/

Provides step-by-step instructions for getting onto the Web. It has links to the necessary software and is primarily for novices but offers some tips for experts.

Netscape Tutorials
http://www.bgsu.edu/departments/tcom/netscape.html

Offers a step-by-step tutorial on how to use one of the finest WWW browsers available, Netscape.

Netscape's Homepage
http://home.netscape.com/

This is Netscape's homepage. You can download Netscape's newest WWW browsers. You can also get Net tutorials and references at this site.

New Surfer's Guide
http://www.imaginarylandscape.com/helpweb/www/oneweb.html

Offers helpful articles on how to tour the Web and understand the terms used. Provides access to some useful starting points.

NSTA Online Resources
http://www.nsta.org/onlineresources/

This site provides extensive links to a variety of on-line resources such as html guides, Internet guides, and other sites that contain a huge collection of science and math lesson plans. You will be able to search on site for the type of resources that you are interested in obtaining.

Resources for New Internet Users
http://www.traverse.com/chartermi_resources/newusers.shtml

This site provides access to a useful Internet tutorial as well as various interesting sites to surf and visit.

The Internet Help Desk
http://www.glowworms.com/~alward/

This free guide helps both beginners and advanced Internet users. Covers e-mail, Netiquette, and browsers.

The Online World Resources Handbook
http://home.eunet.no/~presno/

Offers help with starting points, Web page design, e-mail, and other facets of the Web.

The New Users Directory
http://hcs.harvard.edu/~calvarez/newuser.html

Gives an introductory overview of the Web, features a rough guide to downloading software, and provides links to other starting points.

NARROWING SEARCHES FOR NET-WORTHY SITES

There are many methods of narrowing down your searches when you are surfing the World Wide Web. The methods might differ depending on which search engine and subject directories you are using at the time. In order to get you started, the following few links below will provide you with a good synopsis of how you can progressively conduct a search on the World Wide Web:

Finding Information on The Internet
http://www.lib.berkeley.edu/TeachingLib/Guides/Internet/FindInfo.html

A tutorial from the University of California at Berkeley. The site describes a five-step search strategy which is quite unique:

Step 1 – Analyze your topic to decide where to begin

Step 2 – Pick the right starting place

Step 3 – Learn as you go and VARY your approach with what you learn.

Step 4 – Don't bog down in any strategy that doesn't work.

Step 5 – Return to previous strategies better informed.

Bare Bones 101: A Very Basic Web Search Tutorial
http://www.sc.edu/beaufort/library/bones.html

This site from the University of South Carolina provides definitions, search strategies, and specific information about subject directories and search engines. The table of contents taken from the site is listed below:

Lesson 1: Search Engines: a Definition

Lesson 2: Metasearchers: a Definition

Lesson 3: Subject Directories: a Definition

Lesson 4: Library Gateways and Specialized Databases: a Definition

Lesson 5: Evaluating Web Pages

Lesson 6: Creating a Search Strategy

Lesson 7: Basic Search Tips

Lesson 8: Searching with Boolean Logic and Proximity Operators

Lesson 9: Field Searching

Lesson 10: Troubleshooting

Lesson 11: AltaVista: A Closer Look

Lesson 12: Excite: A Closer Look

Lesson 13: Fast Search: A Closer Look

Lesson 14: Google: A Closer Look

Lesson 15: HotBot: A Closer Look

Lesson 16: Ixquick Metasearch: A Closer Look

Lesson 17: Northern Light: A Closer Look

Lesson 18: Yahoo!: A Closer Look

Lesson 19: Final Exam

Lesson 20: Beyond "Bare Bones"

The Spider's Apprentice
http://www.monash.com/spidap.html

This site describes how search engines work and helps you search the Web more efficiently. It guides you on which search engines are most effective. The table of contents taken from the site is listed below:

Top of Page—A Useful Guide to Web Search Engines

- What's New with Search Engines
- What Spidap Offers
- Our Current Search Engine Rankings

Page Two—Basic Search Engine FAQ
Some Frequently Asked Questions about Web Search. This page will be most useful for Web search beginners.

Page Three—How To Plan The Best Search Strategy
Do you really want a search engine? Have you tried a Web directory like Yahoo first? We'll explain the differences between the two.

Page Four—How Search Engines Work
Explanation of keyword searching, concept based searching, text indexing, query refining (yes—all the Boolean stuff!) and relevancy ranking.

Page Five—The Web Search Wizard
This is our Action Page! Jump straight here for tips on Smart Searching. You can also search the Web directly from our page. And we'll direct you to some specialized databases that will help you find people, phone numbers, company info or just plain fun!

Page Six—In-Depth Analysis of Popular Search Engines
Here we give the details on the most popular Web search engines. We also rank the search engines with letter grades for overall quality and usability.

Pandia Search Central
http://www.pandia.com/goalgetter/index.html

This site provides a guide to web searching, with search engine tutorials, tools, news, and optimization resources. There are also newsfinder and metasearch engine tools embedded on the site. The table of contents taken from the site is listed below:

- Introduction to the search engine tutorial
- What is the Internet anyway?
- What kind of search services should you use?
- Internet directories
- Search Engines
- Metasearch Engines
- Search utilities

- The best search engines and directories
- Advanced Internet Searching – as easy as ordering pizza
- Boolean Operators: AND, AND NOT, OR
- "Phrases"
- Proximity: the NEAR-operator
- Case Sensitivity
- Nesting (Brackets)
- Truncation or wildcards
- Search Engine Maths; the easier way
- Field searching
- Error codes
- Pandia's 17 Recommendations for Internet Searching

Sink or Swim
http://www.ouc.bc.ca/libr/connect96/search.htm

This site provides you with techniques for an Internet search. The site was developed by Okanagan University College Library. The table of contents taken from the site is listed below:

- Introduction
- Search Engines & Subject Directories
- Search Engines
- Multi-Threaded Search Engines
- Subject-specific Search Engines
- Subject Directories
- Specialized Subject Directories
- Search Strategy
- Search Logic
- Boolean Logic
- Search Tips
- Search Engine Comparisons
- Individual search engines:
- AltaVista
- Excite
- FAST
- Google
- HotBot
- Northern Light

- Multi-threaded (meta) search engines:
- Dogpile
- Ixquick
- Metacrawler
- ProFusion
- SurfWax
- Exercises

How to Search the World Wide Web
http://204.17.98.73/midlib/tutor.htm

This site provides a tutorial and guide for beginners. The table of contents taken from the site is listed below:

Basics of Conducting a Search

A. Search Tools and Methods. Describes the means used in conducting a search.

B. Keyword Search Operators. Describes use of operators to compose queries.

C. Search Tools. Lists preferred search tools and their keyword operators.

D. Planning and Conducting a Search. Provides a guide for conducting searches.

E. Hints and Information. Useful facts about the workings of the Internet.

F. Comments and About the Authors.

Advanced Information

G. Search Tool Descriptions. Describes the contents and use of preferred search tools.

H. Conducting Searches. A guide on use of operators and composing queries.

I. Home Page. Explains Home Page and Popular Site contents.

J. Glossary. Defines terms used in the search process.

Summary of Some of the Effective Methods of Conducting a Search

These procedures or techniques will work with most search engines/directories.

1. Include the plus sign (+) and the minus sign (−) in front of the words that you are typing on the search engine in order to force inclusion and/or exclusion in searches.

Example: +science-math

2. Always type in the words that are the main search criteria first in the sentence.

Example: (in this case the word "science" is the main search criterion): +science education in Canada

3. You can use Boolean searches when you type keywords into the search engine. The two Boolean statements most used are "AND" and "OR." The statements must always be capitalized. "OR" statements should also be in parentheses and "AND" statements should be in quotation marks (""). Quotation marks are used to ensure that the search will contain search results with the words side by side (in the case below it is "science education").

Example: "science education" AND (canada OR usa)

4. The wild card sign (*) can also be used to obtain search results that contain a variety of topics starting with the letters of the word that was typed into the search engine.

Example: *sci** will return search results such as scifi, sci/tech, sci.astro.

CHAPTER SUMMARY

We have described what the Internet is and have shown you how to surf the Internet. In this chapter we provided you with some useful Web sites that show you how you can use the search engine effectively and how you can narrow your search as well as identify Net-worthy sites in science. For detailed procedures on surfing, we have referred you to a number of sites where guides and tutorials are available. The choice is yours! Your technical literacy will improve if you master some of the specialized language that has been provided in the appendix. The Internet language is an important tool for communication.

References

Morris, J. L. (1996). *The technology revolution.* (http://www.uvm.edu/~jmorris/comps2.html)

2

THE INTERNET FOR INTERACTIVE LEARNING

- How Do Science Teachers Use the Internet?

- Testing Ideas Using Science Activities

- Taking a Virtual Science Trip

- Participating in Joint Projects

- Chatting, Conferencing, and E-Mail Journal Writing

- Asking Experts

- Collaborating With Scientists

- Sharing Classroom Activities

- Creating Electronic Portfolios

- The Internet as an On-Line Library for Classroom Lessons

Interactive science programs and lessons can be developed with modern computer technologies. Surf the Internet to experience the interactive nature of information. The click of the mouse on a hot line leads you into many different paths. For example, the URL address: http://www.yahoo.com/Science/Education/K_12/ Activities/ shows hundreds of interactive, hierarchical sites in science. Because of the multiple paths and the combination of textual material, graphics, sounds, videos, photographs, images, animation, and 3-D models available, the Internet can be considered interactive. But, could the learning be interactive with computers?

For interactive learning to occur a learner must engage in thinking about what he/she is learning regardless of the medium in which knowledge is presented. Because computers have the added power of providing presentations that are attractively interactive, students may become motivated to engage in learning. Therefore, we consider computer technologies to be potential media for interactive learning. For example, students are currently using the Netscape browser to collect picture files and construct links to interesting sites on their personal homepages. They are also creating bookmark folders, and adding bookmarks. Thus in a science class, a teacher is able to use the Internet for interactive learning.

HOW DO SCIENCE TEACHERS USE THE INTERNET?

Joel Bass, a teacher of science teachers, uses the Internet to help his students collect real time data. Marlene Kroeker, a secondary science teacher, uses the Internet for planning science fairs. Mark Huebert, a secondary science preservice teacher uses the Internet for research. These teachers' experiences with the Internet are described in this section.

Collecting Real Time Data (Joel Bass)

I am currently doing a lab which requires the use of real time tide data from NOAA. Students have to go to San Francisco and other sites to collect data throughout the day. This data is submitted to an on-line database on my machine from which they develop and retrieve data and develop charts and graphs. This type of activity uses the power of the Internet. [Joel Bass, a science teacher educator at Sam Houston University, private correspondence, November, 1997]

The Internet has been an important means for scientists at multiple sites to collaborate in research projects. Just as the Internet has been productive in scientific research, it can be an excellent tool in the science classroom in promoting a constructivist approach to interactive exploration and learning. By bringing interesting and significant information into the classroom, technology can provide effective enrichments that might not be possible otherwise.

The New Jersey Networking Infrastructure in Education (NJNIE) project has taken a lead in developing on-line activities for students (Friedman, Baron, and Addison, 1996). In NJNIE Internet activities, the focus is on analysis of quantitative data that is emerging from current sources. Through working with data from the

Internet, students not only deepen their knowledge of science, they increase their mathematical skills as they encounter the precise order, regularity, and predictability that is inherent in the natural world.

NJNIE has done valuable preliminary work in designing activities that suggest how Internet data sources might be used in science classes. Consider the NJNIE activity on Ships at Sea as an example. If you have Internet available now, you might wish to examine the Ships at Sea site at the URL address: njnie.di-stevens-tech.edu/curriculum/oceans/stowaway.html.

Hundreds of ships in the world's oceans regularly report their precise locations along with basic information about weather and water conditions. Ocean Weather, Inc. maintains a database on this information, updating it several times each day. Ships are designated by IDs; locations of each ship are given by latitude and longitude and can also be seen on an Ocean Graphic map. The sheer volume of data can be overwhelming, but it becomes manageable within the context of engaging students in problems related to vicarious travel. Students pretend they are stowaways on a ship with a given ID. The stowaways wonder where they are going and when they will arrive. Somehow they obtain access to the Internet. Referring to sequential reports of their ship's location given on the Internet, students map their trip and try to predict the location of the port to which the ship is bound. Internet sources linked to the Ships at Sea site can also be used to determine how far the ship has traveled between two specific locations. Using the distance information and time data drawn from the ship's reports, students can calculate the ship's rate of speed. With this information, and calculations of the distance from their current location to the destination port, students can estimate their time of arrival. The whole scenario is presented as a problem, with students having to determine which concepts are relevant and how the concepts are to be used.

Activities somewhat similar to NJNIE's Ships at Sea can be carried out with data on the locations of whales given on the Whale Net Web site. The URL address of this site is

http://whale.wheelock.edu

Source: J. Michael Williamson, Whalenet, Wheelock College.

Similar to the Ships at Sea database, Whale Net provides information on the date and location (latitude and longitude) for each sighting of a right whale named Rat. A black and white map of the ocean is provided for mapping data on Rat's movements. Students can enter the latitude and longitude data for two points on the map into a "distance generator," which is provided at a site linked to Whale Net, and determine how far apart the points are. In an inservice project for middle school math and science teachers, participants were encouraged to formulate and address different questions about Rat's movement. Some questions addressed by the teachers were: What was the maximum distance Rat traveled in one day? What was his maximum speed? Are weather and water conditions related to the fact that Rat seems to linger near particular locations? The teachers worked to answer the questions through analysis of the data available on the Internet.

A great deal of data on sunspots is also available on the Internet. Images of the sun can be studied from the National Oceanographic & Atmospheric Administration's site

www.noaa.gov

Source: NOAA Office of Public Affairs, U. S. Dept. of Commerce.

This site shows sunspots and gives the latitudes and longitudes of their positions on the surface of the sun. NJNIE presents an interesting set of sunspot activities in a Sun Module found on their Web site at www.users.interport.net/-ibaron/solar.html.

Sunspots are dark areas on the sun's surface that appear as a result of concentrated magnetic fields. The sunspots form and dissipate over periods of days or weeks. In one activity, the middle school teachers in the inservice project calculated the average number of sunspots seen each day for each month throughout the last year. Similar data on the average number of sunspots were available on a linked site for every month since the 1950s. The teachers combined this data with their own calculated data and graphed the average number of sunspots for each month over a 40-year period. Through careful analysis of their graphs, the teachers discovered that the average number of sunspots waxes and wanes, reaching a maximum every 11 years.

In a second activity, the teachers used real time sunspot data, available on a gopher site linked to the Sun Module, to calculate the rotational rate of the sun. The teachers selected a particular sunspot (identified by a reference number) and determined its location on the sun for each day over a period of several days. The location is given in terms of the latitude and longitude on the surface of the sun, such as N30W48 (latitude 30 North, longitude 4811 West) The teachers noted that the longitude changed regularly, indicating that the sunspot was moving east to west over time. The teachers calculated that the sunspots were drifting west at a rate of about 1011 to 120 sunspot numbers (mm) per day. Assuming that the spots were fixed on the surface of the sun, they estimated that the sun would make one complete rotation about every 30 days.

The Internet facilitates new types of interesting, intellectually significant educational tasks that are not likely to reach learners via other methods. Through database Internet activities, students at all levels can engage in the constructive types of explorations that are common among scientists.

Canada Geese, Imprinting, Bird Adaptations (Tanis Clayton)

Lesson 1. Assessing students' prior ideas of Canada Geese.

Have students design a web using a visual organizer such as Inspiration to illustrate everything they already know and understand about geese. Save file within class folder of a network or on a floppy disk. Configure network to share files.

Lesson 2. Developing students' collective ideas.

Have students collaborate with peers to access each other's networked file. Students will use Inspiration to create a Venn diagram of students' combined ideas about Canada geese. Students will use copy and paste feature to merge information from the two separate networked or floppy files. They will then save file within class folder of a network or on a floppy disk.

Lesson 3. Surfing websites to study about geese in their natural habitat.

The following websites are quite informative:

True Geese of the World: The Branta Species
http://www.utm.edu/departments/ed/cece/trugeese2.shtml

All About the Majestic Canada Goose
http://www.icu.com/geese/doc2.html

Canada Geese in North America
http://biology.usgs.gov/s+t/noframe/b011.htm

Branta's Place: The Museum of Canada Geese
http://www.canadagoose.com

FAQs: Frequently Ask Questions about Canada Geese
http://www.canadagoose.com/askbranta.html

Lesson 4. Preparing a report on geese after surfing the Web.

Have students create a slide show using MS Power Point or Corel Presentation, Hyperstudio, or MS Publisher Brochure inserting images from the shared networked classrom file or images from the Internet.

Lesson 5. Locating and recording related information in a word processor using a search engine of student choice.

Students will use the following key search words: Bill Lishman, Father Goose, Interview Lishman, Fly Away Home, Branta, Geese. Students will copy and paste only key words from relevant sites into word processor in jot note format. Students will expand notes into sentences and paragraphs later depending upon format of presentation.

Lesson 6. Sustaining students' interest in geese.

Have students play shockwave online game (http://www.spe.sony.com/movies/flyawayhome/index.html) or view the video (Fly Away Home) or read children's novel (*Gumboot Geese,* by Anne Cameron).

Lesson 7. Developing students' e-mail skills.

Have students ask Bill Lishman, fondly known as Father Goose, to communicate with the students focusing on topic of imprinting, making of the movie, or examining information about geese behavior at father.goose@durham.net and ask Branta at doro@monad.net.

Lesson 8. Promoting teamwork in the classroom community.

Students will learn Lessons on Teamwork from Geese at http://www.tpa.org/geese/htm. Students may choose one or more behavioural characterists of the geese and try to reiterate it to their own behaviors. For example, geese honk from behind to encourage those up front to keep up their speed. Using a drawing program or scanned pencil/paper drawings, illustrate the students' interpretations of goose and human teamwork traits. Have students insert illustrations into slide shows, Hyper Studio stacks, brochures, posters, or Web sites.

Lesson 9. Assessing students' understanding of the unit.

Have students write a legend incorporating realistic behaviors of geese. Suggested title is "Why Does the Canada Goose Wear a White Necklace?"

Lesson 10. Extending students' understanding of animal and bird adaptations.

Have students visit the following sites:

Changes in Nesting Behavior of Arctic Geese
http://biology.usgs.gov/s+t/noframe/m8263.htm

Manitoba Animal Wonders
http:/www.mbnet.mb.ca/~assin/ans3.html

Delta Marsh
http://www.umanitoba.ca/faculties/science/delta_marsh/

The Internet for Research (Mark Huebert).

Some of the students initially needed further assistance in finding the Internet browser or entering URLs. Some students wanted more clarification on what was expected of them. However, most students had little difficulty in satisfactorily completing the assignment by the end of the period. The majority of the students stayed on task for most of the period, working hard at completing the assignment. They appeared to enjoy working in pairs, and quietly conversed with one another while searching the Web pages for pertinent information and writing their reports. The change in the learning environment from a regular classroom to the computer lab also seemed to be to the liking of the students. [Mark Huebert, 1997]

I used the Internet for research purposes in my practicum. I had my biology students research the diseases of the digestive system. My lesson plan follows:

Objectives

- To learn about some of the major diseases/disorders of the digestive system
- To become aware of the role society plays in encouraging eating disorders
- To practice using the Internet as a resource for research

Prerequisite Skills

Some basic Windows and Internet skills

Skills Students will Develop

- Using an Internet browser
- Opening Web sites by typing in specific URLs given by the teacher
- Retrieving information about disorders and diseases of the digestive system from the Web sites
- Making a brief about four disorders/diseases of the digestive system using this information

Materials Needed

- PC or compatible, 486 or higher (pentiums preferable). Win 3.1 or above. 8 or more Mb RAM
- Internet browser (e.g., Netscape Navigator, Gold or Internet Explorer)
- Modem (14400 or higher preferable)
- Handout with questions to answer in report, other instructions, and URL addresses

Activity/Procedure

1. Give students the handout (see below) and instruct them to research any four diseases/disorders of the digestive system using the URLs provided, with one of their choices being either bulimia or anorexia.

Handout Given to Students. Internet Sites about Disorders/Diseases of the Digestive System

Your job is to pick four of the disorders/diseases below and write a brief report.

Hepatitis, Cirrhosis, Crohn's Disease, Gallstones, Heartburn, Hemorrhoids, Lactose Intolerance, Ulcers, Colitis, Irritable Bowel Syndrome
http://WWW.niddk.nih.gov/DigestiveDocs.html

Food Poisoning
http://WWW.columbia.edu/cu/healthwise/0641.html

http://WWW.altabates.com/housecalls/FoodPoisoning.html

Lactose Intolerance
http://WWW.niddk.nih.gov/LactoseIntolerance/LactoseIntolerance.html

http://WWW.adelaide.net.au/~ndk/no_milk.htm

Colitis and Crohn's Disease
http://WWW.niddk.nih.gov/

Eating Disorders (Anorexia and Bulimia)
http://members.aol.com/amanbu/index.html

http://WWW.nimh.nih.gov/publicat/eatdis.htm

Diabetes
http://WWW.niddk.nih.gov/diabetesdocs.html

http://WWW.diabetes.com/site

(Once at site, choose: "Newly Diagnosed?", then scroll down to "the basics," then choose "What is diabetes?")

Cholera
http://WWW-leland.stanford.edu/~moore/Cholera.html

http://WWW.cdc.gov/travel/cholera.htm

---

2. Give a brief overview of how to enter in the URLs.

3. Have students work alone or in pairs, but request every student to hand in his/her individual work at the end of the period.

4. Have students share their findings with the class in the next period.

5. Discuss the role of today's society in increasing the incidence of anorexia and bulimia in the West.

Assessment

Assessment will be based on students' effort during Internet search and their final oral and written report about one of the diseases.

Reflection

In this lesson students will direct their own learning with the teacher being the guide and resource person. The computer lab setting will allow me to monitor and interact with individual students with relative ease.

Student Research

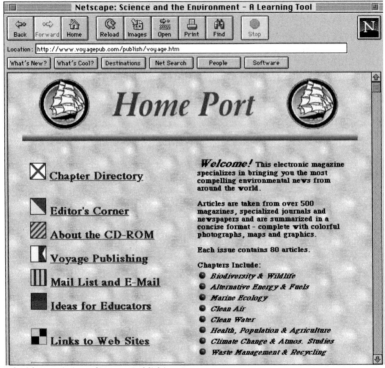

Reprinted with permission of Voyage Publishing, Inc.

Students can have access to scientific information from the Library of Congress' collection, ERIC, journals, magazines, and newspapers. For example, Science and the Environment (http://www.voyagepub.com/publish/voyage.htm) is an electronic magazine which brings the environmental news from all over the world. Articles are taken from over 500 magazines, specialized journals and newspapers. These articles are complete with colorful photographs, maps, and graphics. Scientific information may be also obtained from informal learning institutions such as museums and space agencies. NASA sites (http://quest.arc.nasa.gov/; http://wwwspace.arc.nasa.gov/division/; http://www.nasa.gov/) contain information on all of the space

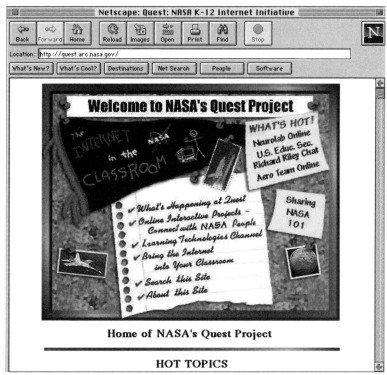

Source: NASA Ames Research Center.

agency's programs, an online library for research, and exhibits on recent space phenomena, such as the comets, Hubble Telescope, MIR, and the Galileo spacecraft.

Although NASA is taking the lead, the National Oceanic and Atmospheric Administration (NOAA), the Department of Energy, the National Institutes of Health (NIH), and many more have good research data available for students to work with once retrieved from the Internet. The butterfly migrations and acid rain projects are seen by educators and the public as two of the most effective uses of the Internet.

Peer Talk: Potential Uses of the Internet

What are some of the other potential uses of the Internet? Describe and give examples.

_____

_____

_____

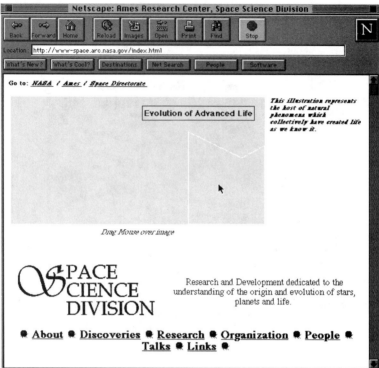

Source: NASA Ames Research Center.

TESTING IDEAS USING SCIENCE ACTIVITIES

In conceptual change models of teaching, both teachers and students must look for activities that may answer some of their questions or test their ideas. Frank Potter's Science Gems—Earth Science (http://www-sci.lib.uci.edu/SEP/earth.html) categorizes more than 2000 earth science links. The Yuckiest Site in the Internet (http://www.nj.com/yucky/) features multimedia classroom activities and information for more than 100 physical science lessons from K-12 in Physical Science Lessons (http://www.eecs.umich.edu/mathscience/funexperiments/agesubject/physicalsciences.html). These lessons and activities, appropriately chosen, can be used to either clarify or elaborate students' conceptions.

Conducting Internet Labs

For the investigation of the cell and photosynthesis, a group of students used URL:http://lenti.med.umn.edu/~mwd/cell_WWW/chapter1/cell_chapter1.html Students examined the information on prokaryotes and eukaryotes and answered the following questions:

1. Compare the eukaryotes with the prokaryotes using the information on the Net. Add it to your notes.

Source: NASA.

2. Find the drawings of the bacterium and cyanophyte. Draw and label these cells.

3. Discuss the cell diagram. Find an organelle that we did not discuss in class. Name this organelle. Click on the organelle and write a brief description of it.

4. How are these organelles not like lysosomes?

5. Click on the rest of the structures on this cell and copy down any information that will help add to your class notes.

6. Find information about the plasma membrane and the function of the cholesterol in the lipid bilayer. (Adapted from Timmons, et al., 1997.)

TAKING A VIRTUAL SCIENCE TRIP

Students can visit a zoo or science center from the classroom even if field trips are not possible. This is what makes the Internet so beneficial. The Internet provides a virtual experience. Adventures, experiments, field trips, and museums are within students' reach through the Internet. The Exploratorium (http://www.exploratorium.edu/learning_studio/news/) is a San Francisco-based interactive science museum which hosts on-line experiments. Students have the experience of

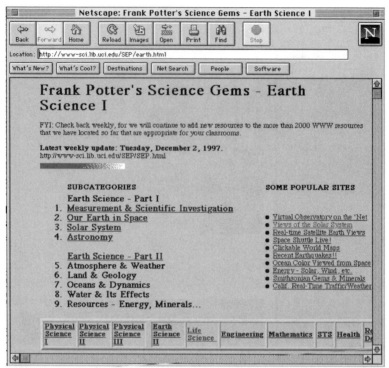

Reprinted with permission of Frank Potter, University of California—Irvine, SEP Assoc. Director.

performing hands-on science at this site (http://www.exploratorium.edu/
light_ walk/pinhole_todo.html). SeaWiFS Project (http://seawifs.gsfc.nasa.gov/
SEAWIFS.html) of NASA's Goddard Space Flight Center provides a teacher's guide
featuring on-line activities with answers for high school students to study ocean
color from space.

PARTICIPATING IN JOINT PROJECTS

Creative Futures (**http://www.ozemail.com.au/~michaels/future.html**)
involves students joining classes around the world in a common classroom project
via computers and the Internet. The program encourages students to write and
draw about the future in society, science, and technology using the technology of
the future. Classrooms are encouraged to share their work using the Internet.

CHATTING, CONFERENCING, AND E-MAIL JOURNAL WRITING

Students can do "science chats" with experts in scientific fields as well as worldwide
peers through listservs, or e-mail discussion groups. There are numerous listservs
where students and teachers can ask questions, share and communicate their

© *New Jersey Online.* The Yuckiest Site on the Internet, front page graphics of Website, at http://www.nj.com/yucky/

common knowledge and interests. Examples of listservs are fish ecology (listserv@searn.sunet.se), educational technology (listserv@msu.edu), elementary education (listserv@ksuvm.bitnet), and multimedia (listserv@unlvm.unl.edu).

In 1997, a Russian class wanted to exchange observations about local plant life with 10–15 American boys and girls. The Russian class's search was as follows:

From: root@licey-kupol.altai.ru
To: iecc@stolaf.edu
Subject: Seeking US secondary class for partnership watching for plants' lives

IECC is an international and intercultural classroom e-mail partnership facility in which primary and secondary teachers exchange ideas with other teachers.

E-Mail Journal Writing has also become a way in which students can share their thoughts, ideas, and questions with their teachers and peers. Both teachers and students must be electronically organized because the e-mail mailboxes can get flooded.

With the emergence of Internet communication software such as Cu-SeeMe, Internet Phone, and Cooltalk, as well as with the companion hardware QuickCam (a small ball-shaped camera for the computer), teachers and students can collaborate through video image live on the Internet. Collaboration as well as sharing of ideas and information can be done swiftly, effectively and cost free.

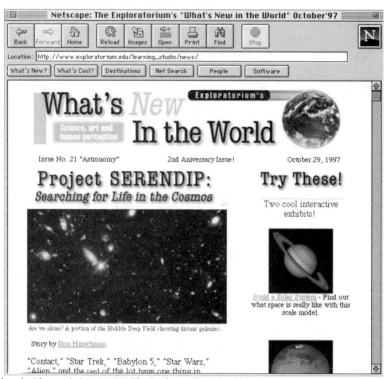

Reproduced with permission. © 1998 The Exploratorium, San Francisco.

ASKING EXPERTS

When students come up with interesting and challenging questions teachers can take the opportunity to direct students to an expert scientist. For example, the Mad Scientist Network (http://medicine.wustl.edu:80/~ysp/MSN/MAD.SCI.html) is a collective cranium of scientists from around the world fielding questions in different areas of science. The scientists answer students' questions based on their homework and research projects. A teacher may also become a member of this network to answer students' questions.

COLLABORATING WITH SCIENTISTS

A teacher can find out about events in his or her science areas. Let's Collaborate (**http://www.gene.com/ae/TSN/**) allows a teacher and his or her students to interact with scientists, teachers, and other classrooms to explore the cutting edge of science. It connects biology teachers with leading researchers from around the USA, linking the research-based community of scientists and science experts with the education-based community of teachers. A teacher may wish to join Let's Collaborate for science seminars, SciTalk discussions, and on-line projects. Earth Systems Science Community Curriculum Testbed (http://www.circles.org/) links

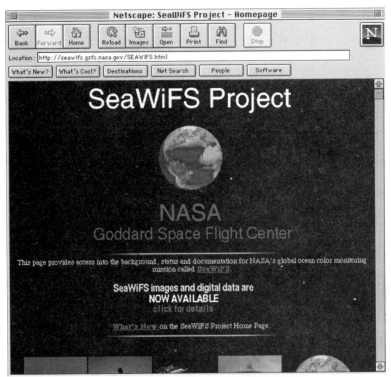

Source: NASA Goddard Space Flight Center.

students and teachers in high schools and universities in an effort to build an earth system science community. This site illustrates how electronic technology can support collaboration among scientists and students.

Students and scientists communicate via e-mail and computer conferencing. This telementoring is useful for project-based teaching and learning. CoVis Project (1993) at Northwestern University provides volunteer telementoring service to secondary students with long-term science projects. Following is an excerpt of an e-mail exchange between a secondary student and a graduate student about earthquake research.

Thursday, 2 May 1996
Dear Mary,
We are juniors at New Trier High School. We are participating in a group project involving earthquakes. Your help would be greatly appreciated. Our project is due on May 17.
Yours Truly, Marilyn and Robert

Dear Marilyn and Robert,
Hello and welcome! Glad to hear from you. I'm really excited about working with you on this project. Whew! Tight time line, but I'm sure we can make it. What

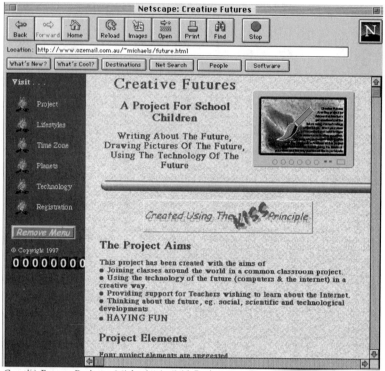

Source. Creative Futures Project—Michael Schofield, Project Coordinator.

aspect of earthquakes are you interested in? We first need to define the question/info that best graphs your interest, and then we can formulate a research attack plan for the project. Draft a few ideas on paper, then e-mail me back with the info. Once we have a good topic, we can hit the ground running. If you're short on ideas, grab the local paper or the Tribune, *or news magazines like* Time, Newsweek, *or even* Discovery. *With the recent earthquake in the Pacific Northwest, I'm sure the media has cooked up a few articles with cool graphics. (O'Neill, Wagner, & Gomez, 1996, p. 39)*

Rich conversation and learning takes place when the projects are challenging and interesting and sufficient time is given to students to complete the project. Teachers recruit telementors by posting a message on the Usenet newsgroups and listservs dedicated to scientific research. Subsequently, teachers describe the project and their expectation of students to the volunteering telementors through e-mail. The success of telementoring depends on the commitment of both the telementee and the telementor, time given to telementors for their feedback to students, and the teacher's on-going communication with the telementor and students.

Reprinted with permission of Washington University School of Medicine.

SHARING CLASSROOM ACTIVITIES

"The World Wide Web (WWW) is the world's largest bulletin board" (Morris, 1996). A teacher may post an original lesson idea or activity on this electronic bulletin board. For example, the Keep America Beautiful Homepage (http://www.kab.org/) provides educational information on solid waste management (recycling, composting, waste-to-energy, sanitary, landfilling) and litter prevention. It also offers lesson plans and other publications on-line. For alternative assessment, visit Miami Museum of Science—Alternative Assessment (http://www. miamisci.org:80/ph/lpexamine1.html). Types of alternative assessment presented in this site are performance-based, authentic or project, portfolio, and journal. Each of these types of assessment is graphically illustrated by using The pH Factor. Within the journal section, Howard Gardner's theory of multiple intelligence is illustrated.

CREATING ELECTRONIC PORTFOLIOS

An electronic portfolio is an interactive multimedia approach to organizing learning experiences in the on-line environment. Teachers use multimedia software such as HyperStudio, Hypercard, and Kid Pix to create and manage an electronic portfolio.

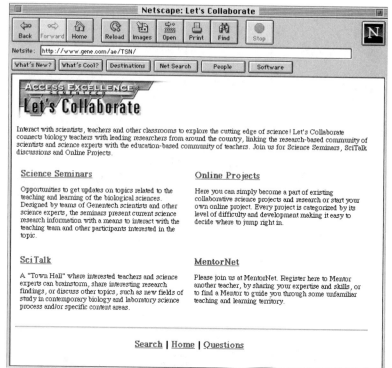

Reprinted with permission of Genentech, Inc.

Portfolios can include text, graphics, sound, animation, and video to represent as well as share what you have learned. My Portfolio Reflection (http://ucsu.colorado.edu:80/~strother/port.html) is an example of an electronic portfolio. FoxFire Electronic Portfolio (http://mailer.fsu.edu:80/~jflake/assign.html) outlines principles and suggestions for developing an electronic portfolio. Why Electronic Portfolio Assessment? (http://www.cs.binghamton.edu:80/~loland/why.html) discusses the benefits of electronic portfolio assessment as well as ideas for managing portfolios.

THE INTERNET AS AN ON-LINE LIBRARY FOR CLASSROOM LESSONS

The Internet has now become the most sought-out on-line library. Science learning becomes real and alive with the Internet. You should be able to use the Internet as well as help your students use the Internet. Learn how to define what you are looking for, how to locate it, how to evaluate it, and how to use it effectively to communicate with others (Morris, 1996).

"Students really need someone to help them define their purpose and steer through the vast amount of material online" (Crawford Kilian in O'Neil, 1996, p. 15).

Source: Ecologic Corporation.

With the use of the Internet's resources teachers can put into practice Howard Gardner's theory of multiple intelligences very effectively, thus meeting the needs and interests of students. Students do not have to be locked into space, time, and resources. For example, Updegrove (1995) reports in the Apple Classrooms of Tomorrow (ACOT) research project in which high school students had many opportunities to use computers and networks to enhance their learning:

> . . . students had significant growth in their independence and their ability to be collaborative problem solvers and communicators. . . . Teachers have shifted their educational approach from one of knowledge transfer (instructionism) to one of knowledge building (constructivism). Classroom instruction shifted from traditional lecture model to one that depended heavily on student collaboration and peer teaching (Apple Education Research Series, summary as cited in Updegrove, 1995).

Computers put the students in the ACOT project in contact with resources worldwide. The teacher's responsibility for stimulating students' interest in a subject still remains—teachers guiding students' thinking about a subject—challenging students to be creative in their approaches to analyzing the topic at hand. The teacher is a mentor and plays an interactive role with his or her students.

Reprinted with permission of Keep America Beautiful, Inc.

A Lesson Example: Introduction to the Anishnabae Clan System Through the Study of Canadian Animals and Their Habitats (Christine Carbotte)

Overview

The Anishnabae (Ojibway) of Canada and the United States have been and still are very connected to our biosphere, as well as the three abiotic spheres of our planet. The traditional and contemporary knowledge gained from life in the boreal forest of the Canadian Shield and their subsequent forced migration into the mixed wood-lands and prairie regions has left the Anishnabae with much to offer the global community. The science and culture of this ancient Algonquin speaking nation has withstood the tests of time, colonial onslaught, the Canadian Indian Act and its many reforms. Their clan systems have survived and still offer a framework for government, social order, and spiritual teachings.

Specific Learning Outcomes

- Use appropriate vocabulary related to their investigations of habitats and communities.

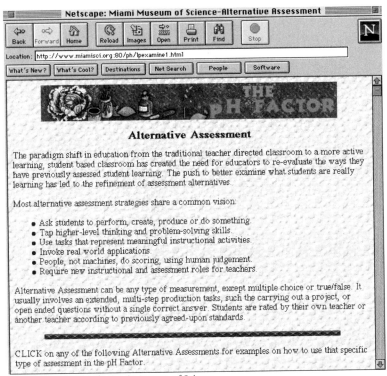

Reprinted with permission of Miami Museum of Science.

- ■ Recognize that each plant and animal depends on a specific habitat to meet its needs.
- ■ Investigate alternate explanations of plant or animal adaptations based on traditional knowledge from a variety of sources.
- ■ Recognize that plant and animal populations interact within a community.

General Learning Outcomes

- ■ Students will be able to identify the factors that affect health and explain the relationships among personal habits, lifestyle choices, and human health, both individual and social.
- ■ Students will be able to employ effective communication skills and utilize information technology to gather and share scientific and technological activities.
- ■ Students will be able to understand essential life structures and processes pertaining to a wide variety of organisms, including humans.
- ■ Students will be able to understand various biotic and abiotic components of ecosystems, as well as their interaction and interdependence within ecosystems and within the biosphere as a whole.

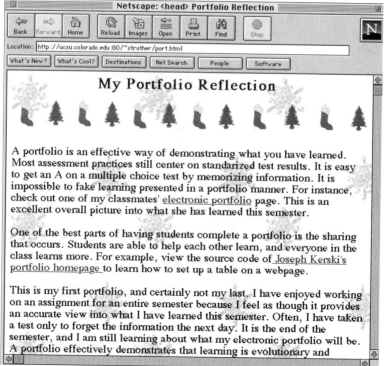

Reprinted with permission of Cheri Strothers, University of Colorado.

Introduction

The Ojibway clan system has evolved over time to accommodate growth and changes. In the beginning there were seven. Some categorizations of this successful community organization would look a little different than others. Still, the major clan functions were to provide for the elements of leadership, defense, sustenance, learning, and medicine; they would remain the same. The list that is provided by Ojibway historians such as William Warren in *History of the Ojibway* is quite extensive compared to others. The following is a partial list of animals that a class of twenty can use to learn about basic societal responsibilities and the clans that traditionally take care of them.

Leadership—Eagle, hawk, crane, goose, loon

Learning—Catfish, sturgeon, whitefish

Defense—Bear, wolf, lynx, marten

Sustenance—Beaver, moose, caribou, deer, muskrat

Medicine—Turtle, otter, frog

Teachers may have to add more animals, to meet the number of students in a class; this is acceptable as long as the species is grouped into the suitable category.

Guided Practice

1. Divide the students up into five groups that will represent the societal responsibilities within a community. To do this, pass out cards containing the name of an animal or "clan" to each student from a large envelope, with each name color-coded so the students know which societal responsibility is served by the animal they will be researching. The Web site where they will find some relevant information on their animal should also be on this card.

   While the students are seated in their groups, read the story "How the Fly Saved the River" by Ril Gaiashk. Retrieve it at http://www.ozemail.com.au/ reed/glabal/howthe.html. Have students open up http://www.geocities.com/ Athens/Acropolis/5579/ojibwa.html (under Ojibway Spirituality) to view and listen to a three-minute Quick Time video on some history by anthropologist Frances Densmore. See movie 3.

2. Have students open http://www.nald.ca/CLR/chikiken/page23.htm to read how eagles and loons have separate categories according to different people. What is important is that they have leadership responsibilities. Students should record relevant information about the attributes and responsibilities of their particular animal. Click on Customs and Beliefs, then the table of contents. Have them scroll down and open the file entitled Life After European Contact—Manitoba Lifestyle: Economic Pursuits. Have students carefully read the seven types of occupations and have them summarize the topic that most suits their "community responsibility." They must explain why their "clan" should be responsible for this pursuit. The responsibilities should be divided up to look like this: Hunting/trapping—sustenance, Fishing—learning, Guiding—leadership, Manitoba maple sugar/wild rice—defense, and Seneca root—medicine. Have students brainstorm on different occupations that each group would be most suitable for in order to support their families today. For example, Turtle clan people might easily become doctors or chiropractors, Sturgeons might become teachers or Bears might become law enforcers. Be aware that aboriginal people today do not necessarily choose a profession according their clan attribute, but this is often the case.

3. Have students open http://www.turtle-island.com/traditions.html, then scroll down to Turtle clan. They need to read this to learn more about their clan and responsibilities.

4. Have students do research with the Internet on the specific animal that they have been assigned to learn about. Essential facts should include information such as habitat (boreal forest, broadleaf, or mixed), food, vital statistics, reproduction, and at least five additional facts.

   Eagle—http://www.cws-scf.ec.gc.ca/hww-fap/bald/bald.html

   Hawk—http://www.hawkwatch.org/spotlight.htm

   Crane—http://species.fws.gov/bio_whoo.html

   Goose (Canada)—http://www.icu.com/geese/doc2.html

Loon—http://www.cws-scf.ec.gc.ca/hww-fap/loons/loons.html

Whitefish—http://www.dfo-mpo.gc.ca/COMMUNIC/ss-marin/coregone/white.htm

Bear—http://www.schoolnet.ca/vp-pv/mammals/e/list8.html

Wolf—http://www.schoolnet.ca/vp-pv/mammals/e/pg190.html

Lynx—http://www.schoolnet.ca/vp-pv/mammals/e/pg20.html

Marten—http://www.schoolnet.ca/vp-pv/mammals/e/pg235.html

Beaver—http://www.schoolnet.ca/vp-pv/mammals/e/list24.html

Moose—http://www.schoolnet.ca/vp-pv/mammals/e/pg214.html

Caribou—http://www.schoolnet.ca/vp-pv/mammals/e/pg94.html

Deer—http://www.schoolnet.ca/vp-pv/mammals/e/pg18.html

Muskrat—http://www.schoolnet.ca/vp-pv/mammals/e/pg12.html

Turtle—http://www.geocities.com/Heartland/Prairie/1454/info.html

Otter—http://www.schoolnet.ca/vp-pv/mammals/e/pg87.html

Frog—http://allaboutfrogs.org

5. Have students open up http://endangered.fws.gov/kids/biodivrs.htm and record a definition of bio-diversity.

6. After all the information has been gathered, have a sharing circle with the students. Within this circle they should be seated with their research groups. Have each student read his or her information for the rest of the "mini-clan system" that sits in the circle.

Evaluation

Check to make sure that all the information in the research booklets is correct. The students will write a creative writing story about the animal they researched. All the information they gathered in the research assignment should be included in their stories.

Relevant Sites

Aboriginal Science Projects
http://www.schoolnet.ca/aboriginal/science2/index-e.html

Animal games and crosswords.
http://endangered.fws.gov/kids/risky.htm

Bird Migration Facts
http://north.audubon.org/facts.html

Oral traditions—turtle clan
http://www.turtle-island.com

A comprehensive site on Anishnabae culture—historical and contemporary issues. Oral traditions—turtle clan is very relevant for this lesson.

Canadian Wildlife Service-Hinterland Who Is Who
http://www.cws-scf.ec.gc.ca/hww-fap/eng_ind.htm

Endangered Means There Is Still Time
http://www.nbs.gov/features/kidscorner/

Environmental Web Resources
http://www.cee-ane.org/www/index.html

Green Teacher—Education for Planet Earth
http://www.web.ca/-greentea/

Listen to six different moose calls
http://www.fieldandstream.com/hunting/biggame/moosecalls/

Native American Indian Resources (Aboriginal science, herbal knowledge, and astronomy)
http://indy4.fdl.cc.mn.us/~isk/mainmenue.html

Ontario Field Ornithologists—Ontario Bird Checklist
http://www.interlog.com/~ofo/chcklst.htm

Power Symbols—Honoring the Animal Spirits
http://www.powersource.com/gallery/objects/default.html

The Environmental Education
http://envirolink.org/enviroed/envirok12.html

U.S. Fish and Wildlife Species—Wildlife Fact Sheets
http://species.fws.gov/

Wild Wings Heading North—Track Snow Geese on the Net
http://north.audubon.org/

CHAPTER SUMMARY

The Intenet has now become the most sought-out on-line library. Science education becomes real and alive with the Internet. A virtual travel to the Smithsonian Institute will enable us to stop and explore the characteristics of many interesting gems and minerals. *We* should be able to use the Internet as well as help *our students* use the Internet. We as well as our students must learn "how to define what we are looking for, how to locate it, how to evaluate it, and how to use it effectively to communicate with others" (Morris, 1996). It has been projected that by the year 2000 every school in North America will be connected to the Internet. Teachers and students who do not use the Internet will be left behind in the stream of technology!

References

Friedman, E. A., Baron, J. D., & Addison, C. J. (1996). Universal access to science study via Internet. *THE Journal* (Technological Horizons in Education), *23*(11), 83–86.

Kroeker, M. (1997). It's science fair time. *The Manitoba Science Teacher;* *39* (2), 33–35.

Morris, J. L. (1996). *The technology revolution.* (http://www.uvm.edu/~jmorris/comps2.html)

Timmons, V., Liu, X., Macmillan, R., MacDonald, L., & MacKinnon, R. (1997). *Integration of Technology into Secondary Curriculum: Stage Two—Appendixes.* Antigonish, Nova Scotia: The Office of Learning Technologies, St. Francis Xavier University.

Updegrove, K. H. (1995). *Teaching on the Internet.* (http://pobox.upenn.edu/~kimu/teaching.html)

3

LINKS TO SCIENCE ACTIVITIES

- Addressing the Science Content Standards
- Earth and Space Science
- Life Science
- Physical Sciences
- General Science
- Elementary Science
- Secondary Science
- K–12 Science
- Science, Technology, and Society Connections
- Integrating Science and Other Curricular Areas

ADDRESSING THE SCIENCE CONTENT STANDARDS

The American Association for the Advancement of Science (AAAS, 1989), the National Research Council (NRC, 1996), the Pan Canadian Curricular Frameworks (1997), and the Third International Mathematics and Science Study (TIMSS, 1994) outline recommendations for developing scientific literacy, "a more valid way to know how science works; a better sense of inquiry and its dependency on human need and discourse" (Ebenezer & Connor, 1998). In particular, the National Research Council outlines a set of science content standards and expects these to be a complete set of outcomes for students: "What students should know, understand, and be able to do in natural science" (NRC, 1996). These standards are:

- Science as inquiry
- Unifying concepts and processes in science
- Physical science
- Life science
- Earth and space science
- Science and technology
- Science in personal and social perspectives
- History and nature of science

Science concepts that are critical for every K–12 student are identified in Tables 3-1, 3-2, and 3-3 (National Research Council, 1996, pp. 109–111).

As you examine these content standards, consider how the Internet plays a role in developing scientific literacy. How does the Internet help "live out" the National Science Standards for teaching, learning, and assessment? Consider the Web sites in the following sections. The info-bar that will be used is shown below:

R	GL	TCK	RR	STS	IL	RTD

R	Rating (* = Average, ** = Very Good)	STS	Science, Technology, and Society
GL	Grade Level		
TCK	Teacher Content Knowledge	IL	Inquiry Lessons
RR	Research Reports	RTD	Real-Time Data

EARTH AND SPACE SCIENCE

An Astronomy Course for Middle/High School Students
http://darkskyinstitute.org/astronomy.html

This site provides an astronomy course for middle/high school students using the Internet. Information is well presented with key hyperlinks to more effective content areas. Topics available in this Web site include:

- STARGZR, Sparkling Eyes, Happy Grins
- Observing the Night Sky

Table 3-1 Content Standards, Grades K–4			
Unifying Concepts and Processes	**Science as Inquiry**	**Physical Science**	**Life Science**
Systems, order, and organization Evidence, models, and explanation Change, constancy, and measurement Evolution and equilibrium Form and function	Abilities necessary to do scientific inquiry Understandings about scientific inquiry	Properties of objects and materials Position and motion of objects Light, heat, electricity, and magnetism	Characteristics of organisms Life cycles of organisms Organisms and environments
Earth and Space Science	**Science and Technology**	**Science in Personal and Social Perspectives**	**History and Nature of Science**
Properties of earth materials Objects in the sky Changes in earth and sky	Abilities of technological design Understandings about science and technology Abilities to distinguish between natural objects and objects made by humans	Personal health Characteristics and changes in populations Types of resources Changes in environments Science and technology in local challenges	Science as a human endeavor

Reprinted with permission from the National Research Council (1996). *National Science Education Standards.* Washington, D.C.: National Academy Press.

- ■ Light Pollution
- ■ Finding Your Way Around the Sky
- ■ Messages From the Cosmos
- ■ Binoculars and Telescopes
- ■ The Moon
- ■ The Sun
- ■ The Solar System
- ■ Stars, Nebulae, and Star Clusters
- ■ Galaxies and Quasars

Table 3-2   Content Standards, Grades 5–8

Unifying Concepts and Processes	Science as Inquiry	Physical Science	Life Science
Systems, order, and organization Evidence, models, and explanation Change, constancy, and measurement Evolution and equilibrium Form and function	Abilities necessary to do scientific inquiry Understandings about scientific inquiry	Properties and changes of properties in matter Motions and forces Transfer of energy	Structure and function in living systems Reproduction and heredity Regulation and behavior Population and ecosystems Diversity and adaptations of organisms

Earth and Space Science	Science and Technology	Science in Personal and Social Perspectives	History and Nature of Science
Structure of the earth system Earth's history Earth in the solar system	Abilities of technological design Understandings about science and technology	Personal health Populations, resources, and environments Natural hazards Risks and benefits Science and technology in society	Science as a human endeavor Nature of science History of science

Reprinted with permission from the National Research Council (1996). *National Science Education Standards.* Washington, D.C.: National Academy Press.

■ Cosmology

■ Other Really Cool Astrostuff

■ Who Writes This Stuff Anyway?

R	GL	TCK	RR	STS	IL	RTD
*	7–12	*				*

Table 3-3   Content Standards, Grades 9–12

Unifying Concepts and Processes	Science as Inquiry	Physical Science	Life Science
Systems, order, and organization Evidence, models, and explanation Change, constancy, and measurement Evolution and equilibrium Form and function	Abilities necessary to do scientific inquiry Understandings about scientific inquiry	Structure of atoms Structure and properties of matter Chemical reactions Motions and forces Conservation of energy and increase in disorder Interactions of energy and matter	The cell Molecular basis of heredity Biological evolution Interdependence of organisms Matter, energy, and organization in living systems Behavior of organisms

Earth and Space Science	Science and Technology	Science in Personal and Social Perspectives	History and Nature of Science
Energy in the earth system Geochemical cycles Origin and evolution of the earth system Origin and evolution of the universe	Abilities of technological design Understandings about science and technology	Personal and community health Population growth Natural resources Environmental quality Natural and human-induced hazards Science and technology in local, national, and global challenges	Science as a human endeavor Nature of scientific knowledge Historical perspectives

Reprinted with permission from the National Research Council (1996). *National Science Education Standards.* Washington, D.C.: National Academy Press.

Athena Homepage
http://athena.wednet.edu/

NASA and Science Applications International Cooperation (SAIC) feature a collection of on-line K–12 science lessons and instructional materials on oceans, earth resources, weather and atmosphere, and space and astronomy. For example, the lesson on hurricanes begins with journal writing, asking students to write what they know about hurricanes. The lessons consist of student activities and sheets, task cards, interdisciplinary projects, and further reading. The lessons have ample illustrations, and elementary school students will find it easy to read and follow the instructions.

R	GL	TCK	RR	STS	IL	RTD
**	K–12	*			*	*

Used with permission of edHelper.com

Edhelper.com
http://www.edhelper.com/cat44.htm

The Edhelper.com site includes a wide variety of lesson plans and lesson activities for mathematics and science for all grade levels. The material includes papers and technical information that students could use as resources for research projects in higher grades. The organization of the page is somewhat confusing initially but after a little exploration, a teacher will find a wide variety of resources to build a new class or supplement existing ones. Some of the environmental articles include:

- Global Environmental Change : This article addresses changes in climate that are due to the burning of fossil fuels and the resulting greenhouse effect.

- How Oceans Influence Climate : The long and short term influence of the oceans upon the earth's climate is discussed.

- Is the Earth Warming Up Yet? : Climate models and their accuracy in predicting climate changes are discussed in this article.

Worksheets and testing materials are available for all levels of mathematics and vocabulary education.

R	GL	TCK	RR	STS	IL	RTD
*	K–12	*	**	**	**	

Cool Science Resources
http://hs.scott1.k12.in.us/Resources/Science.htm

Jenna Burrell provides resource materials in astronomy, biology, chemistry, ecology, geology, meteorology, physics, and zoology. The subject matter provided in this site is very useful for students who are preparing for national examinations. For the teacher, Burrell provides in-depth background knowledge that will spur ideas for discussing science-related societal issues. Students will find this site very useful for research reports. This site also provides an e-mail facility to chat with experts in the field and links to other sites for both teachers and students.

■ Astronomy provides a virtual tour of the universe and includes information about each planet as well as many NASA expeditions. Stars and Galaxies has a multimedia approach to astronomy with movies and sound clips.

■ Chemistry provides an interactive table of elements and is very suitable for the preparation of AP and IB tests.

■ Ecology deals with science and the environment. There is a collection of articles about current environmental issues, and papers from the UN are available. This is an important site to visit if you are interested in issue-based teaching.

R	GL	TCK	RR	STS	IL	RTD
**	9–12	*	*	*		

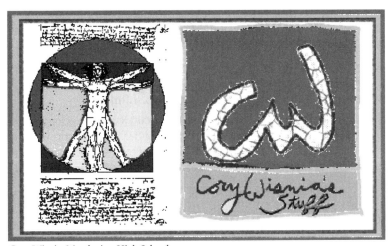

Source: Cory Wisnia. Mendocino High School.

Cory's World (Wizard's World)
http://www.mcn.org/ed/CUR/cw/cwhome.html

Cory's World is a wizard's world that contains illustrative downloadable lessons and units (including games) and other on-line science resources for the study of astronomy and earth science in grades 3–8. This site includes listservs, projects, student-created stacks and Web pages, science poetry page, and kids' corner. The listservs are for science educators, and subscription will provide "updates on grants, curriculum, new or interesting science WWW sites, collaborative project updates from all over." This site is for students who can write and want to publish their own poetry about science-related topics, from nature observations to environmental topics to astronomy and earth science. Kids' Corner is "a place kids may wish to go to find neat sites for on-line interactive science!" You will read about a first-grade teacher who taught a thematic unit on birds. This teacher connected with 18 bird enthusiasts/experts around the USA and had her students send e-mail questions to them. A partial list of Science Education WWW URLs is available.

R	GL	TCK	RR	STS	IL	RTD
**	3–8	*	*	*	*	*

Reprinted with permission of Denver Earth Science Project.

Denver Earth Science Project
http://www.mines.edu/Outreach/Cont_Ed/desp.shtml

The Denver Earth Science Project (DESP) is a K–12 curriculum development effort coordinated by the Colorado School of Mines. In partnership with corporations, federal agencies, school districts, and other institutions of higher education, a series of educational modules addressing a range of earth science topics has been developed:

1. Oil and Gas Exploration—grade level: 7–12
2. Ground Water Studies—grade level: 7–9
3. Paleontology and Dinosaurs—grade level: 7–10
4. Energy: A Closer Look at Oil and Gas—grade level: 4–6
5. Do You Know Your 3 Rs? Radiation, Radioactivity, and Radon—grade level: 7–10

These modules deal with critical issues facing society and are prepared by trained curriculum development teams composed of experienced earth science teachers and practicing scientists. The key to the success of the Project is the involvement of teachers in the design and writing of the materials. Each module is designed to incorporate input from teachers and industrial/governmental partners to assure technical accuracy and relevance to current situations. These modules may be obtained by writing to the Colorado School of Mines.

R	GL	TCK	RR	STS	IL	RTD
*	7–12	*	*	*	*	*

Graphic used with permission of its creator, Chris Rowan.

Educational Space Simulations Project
http://riceinfo.rice.edu/armadillo/Simulations/

This site is an outcome of the Educational Space Simulations Project sponsored by the Houston Independent School District and Rice University. "The purpose of this Web site is to promote the development of education via simulation. Although the primary focus of this site is space simulations, the concept of education via simulation is applicable to a wide range of disciplines."

This site provides resources and links to sites containing activities, lessons, and space simulations. Samples of student astronaut applications consist of an essay and an experimental proposal. You will see pictures of student-generated space simulation that show how to generate a weather report when participating in an educational space simulation.

This site is connected to other sites that are useful to space simulating educators. For example, this site is connected to educational materials available at Discovery Channel School and makes "links to articles, images, audio files, and animations regarding the discovery that life may have existed on Mars 3.6 billion years ago." Some of the important sites are:

- WeatherNet
- Space Shuttle Homepage
- Microsoft Space Simulator

- NASA Educational Workshop for Elementary School Teachers
- NASA and Other Aerospace Centers
- Quest's Online Interactive Projects
- NASA's Spacelink
- NASA's Shuttle-Mir Homepage
- Yahoo! K–12 Sites
- QUEST: NASA's K–12 Initiative
- The Galileo Homepage
- NASA Homepage
- Spacelink Teacher Resource Center
- The Institute for Space and Terrestrial Science
- NASA Education
- Planetariums on the Net

R	GL	TCK	RR	STS	IL	RTD
**	K–12	*	*	*	*	*

Reprinted with permission of Hawaii Space Grant Consortium.

Exploring Planets in the Classroom: Hands-On Activities
http://www.spacegrant.hawaii.edu/class_acts/index.html

Hawaii Space Grant Consortium's Exploring Planets in the Classroom Hands-on Activities was produced by scientists working with local teachers. This site provides more than 25 hands-on science activities in classroom-ready pages for both teachers and students for exploring geology, earth, the planets, and space sciences. These on-line activity pages are formatted for printing and direct classroom use. These resources are an outcome of annual summer courses in Planetary Geosciences offered at the University of Hawaii at Manoa for the state's K-12 teachers and librarians under the direction of Dr. G. Jeffrey Taylor. Hands-on activities in this course are developed and/or tested by the Hawaii Space Grant Consortium in cooperation with teachers statewide. Buttons on this site lead to activities such as:

■ Intro. to the Solar System

■ Planetary Properties

■ Volcanology

■ Impact Craters

■ The Dynamic Earth

■ Gradation

■ Gravity Forces and Rockets

■ The Moon

■ Remote Sensing

Planetary Science Research Discoveries' educational site is devoted to sharing the fascinating discoveries being made by NASA-sponsored planetary scientists. This site is a vital link for education, planetary research, and learning how science works.

This site connects to a National Science Teachers Association list of science and math links, NASA Space Link's electronic information system for educators.

R	GL	TCK	RR	STS	IL	RTD
*	6–12	*	*	*	*	

Frank Potter's Science Gems—Earth Science
http://www.sciencegems.com/earth.html
http://www.sciencegems.com/earth2.html

Frank Potter categorizes more than 2,000 earth science links that are appropriate for your classroom and continues to add new resources weekly. Some popular sites are:

1. Measurement and Scientific Investigation

2. Our Earth in Space

3. Solar System

4. Astronomy

5. Atmosphere and Weather

6. Land and Geology

7. Oceans and Dynamics

8. Water and Its Effects

9. Resources—Energy, Minerals . . .

You will see:

■ Virtual Observatory on the Net

■ Views of the Solar System

- Real-Time Satellite Earth Views
- Space Shuttle Live!
- Clickable World Maps
- Weather Report Worldwide
- Recent Earthquakes!!
- Ocean Color Viewed From Space
- Energy—Solar, Wind, etc.
- Smithsonian Gems and Minerals
- California Real-Time Traffic/Weather

This site offers resources for K–12 on the following subjects:

- Physical Science I
- Physical Science II
- Life Science
- Engineering
- Mathematics
- STS
- Health

For example, kindergarten is the minimum level for Earth Science—Techniques: Measurement and Scientific Investigation.

There are K–12 lesson plans and background material on student reasoning or critical thinking by R. Paul. The minimum level is 3rd grade.

This site includes Exploratorium Science Snackbook of Science Demonstrations—Exploratorium, San Francisco: a sample of about 20 "snacks" from the 100 in the book for simply constructing and investigating science, from optical illusions to electricity and light. Examples are colored shadows and hand battery.

In Scientific Investigation by L. Ginsberg and K. Essani, Western Michigan University: "Students are introduced here to the basis of scientific investigation. Making hypotheses and predictions, identifying components of experimental design, and data collection are performed in the lab. This Web page helps students with some common problems encountered with components of the experimental design, as well as how to present data (graphs and charts) and write a discussion." Some of the other sites that this site is connected to are as follows:

The Franklin Institute Science Museum. There are virtual exhibits (Ben Franklin—Glimpses of the Man; The Heart: A Virtual Exploration); educational hotlists; lessons on energy, geology, health, space science, virtual exhibits, weather science; and a virtual exhibit hotlist with links to many other exhibits and places. Examples include Heart: Sizing Up; B. Franklin as a Scientist; and View of the Moon—Lorenzo in Italy.

Exploring Planets in the Classroom. This site presents hands-on activities from SpaceGrant Consortium at the University of Hawaii at Manoa. Dozens of lesson plans on the solar system, planets, Dynamic Earth, volcanoes, impact craters, the moon, and remote sensing are included.

SeaWiFS Project Ocean Image Archive. (G. C. Feldman at NASA.) This site has pictures and temperature maps plus Earth observation movies. Examples are Global Biosphere, Earth Observation Movies, and Sea Surface Temperatures.

In Amazonia From Space you will find LANDSAT images used by PRODES (the Brazilian Amazon Deforestation Survey Project) in 1991. The minimum grade level is 9th grade. Newton's Apple Educational Materials. The site has more than 100 lessons and teacher guides for the 9th through 13th grades from brain mapping to bread chemistry to the Hubble telescope to printing money to a raptor hospital. Activities, questions, and further investigation suggestions are included. The minimum grade level is 6th grade.

Lightning!! by P. J. Meyer and J. E. Arnold at NASA covers all you want to know about lightning including movies from the Space Shuttle missions, city lights at night from space, storm cells, and rainfall.

Current Weather in U.S. Cities by P. Neilley at NCAR Weather has updates for hundreds of U.S. cities selected via maps or by text.

Weather by WedNet from NASA and SAIC includes lessons about hurricanes, clouds, weather charting, storms from space, precipitation, weather around the world, and some background material. Plenty of images and teacher discussion guides are available. The minimum level is 6th grade.

Live from Antarctica—Passport to Knowledge Project Penguin contains images, hole in the ozone data, and links for teachers and students.

Smithsonian Gem and Mineral Collection. (Photos by D. A. Penland.) This site has about 100 marvelous pictures.

Family Science and Technology Activities from Eduzone at Plymouth Public Schools has dozens of brief lesson plans for the family and children to investigate plants and animals in their neighborhood, seeds and plants, the family tree, rocks, matter, light, and technology.

Virtual Antarctica includes TerraQuest maps, a virtual journey, pictures of the animals in the ocean around Antarctica, and a ship's log for the journey.

Virtual Fantastic Forest has National Geographic Maps, a virtual journey, and pictures of the animals and their habitats in the forest.

Electronic Gemstone Library from the Canadian Institute of Gemology: "[These] gemstones are the more popular ones usually set in jewelry found in retail stores."

Gemology and Lapidary. This site by J. F. Miller Multimedia (text and images) is a very large database on Gemology. Gemology and Lapidary includes the Rainbow of Gems (a list of gems); How are gems classified?; and How are gems cut and polished?

Acid Rain Resources from EcoNet (select acid rain from the list) includes numerous resource links for the waters of the seas, oceans, and rivers and links to acid rain research lessons.

Acid Rain Index to Resources by the Department of the Environment, Canada, has frequently asked questions about acid rain and numerous resource links.

Building a Solar House in Maine. (CREST by W. Lord.) Here you will find the continuing story of a new solar home—how it is being built and how it is working. Also, tables of solar radiation and climate data for comparison and calculation uses are included. Minimum level: 9th grade.

Energy Resources. (CREST by C. Gronbeck.) This site discusses energy resources from solar, wind power, small hydro, geothermal, and biomass and includes global impacts, economics, case studies, history, science concepts, and applications.

R	GL	TCK	RR	STS	IL	RTD
Best	K–16	*	*	*	*	*

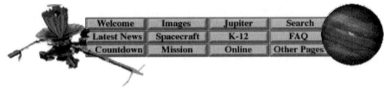

Source: Jet Propulsion Lab, NASA.

Galileo K-12 Educator's Resources
http://www.jpl.nasa.gov/galileo/educator.html

Galileo's Educational Outreach Office produces curriculum units, slide sets, and background sheets to add to your science lesson plans and to help your students keep up on current events when Galileo's mission is in the news. This promotes students' interest in solar system exploration. If you're a parent and your child's teacher doesn't have WWW access, you may consider downloading and printing out copies of any of the materials that you find here for use in your child's classroom. It also provides a layperson's explanation of the term *gravity assist.*

Online From Jupiter is for those who are interested in exploring the solar system or Jupiter and are curious about what it's like working behind the scenes on NASA's Galileo mission. You can peek over the shoulders of Galileo's scientists and engineers and read their responses to questions asked by K–12 students and teachers. Online also features classroom activities, journals, and more.

Music of the Spheres consists of songs contributed by the Galileo team to commemorate important mission events.

Teacher Contributions are some ways in which various teachers have utilized Galileo in their classrooms:

"Hey Kid, Want to Go to Jupiter?" (by Ron Rosano at rosano@well.com) gives your students a brief practical look at how to get a spacecraft to Jupiter. An explanation of gravity assists is suggested prior to doing the activity.

More links for educators are as follows:

Basics of Space Flight Tutorial is a higher-level overview of NASA Spacelink that includes tons of material and conferences for educators.

Welcome to the Planets, a pictorial tour of the solar system.

JPL Educational Outreach is a comprehensive listing of NASA Education links. Galileo Probe Educational Resources are educational briefs.

The Observatorium, NASA's Remote Sensing Public Access Center, contains exhibits that help explain the mysteries of remote sensing in student-friendly terms. (See especially Learning Without Touching.)

Other Resources and Opportunities lists several non-Galileo-specific opportunities, resources, and programs that you may want to investigate.

Hardcopy versions of any educational resource may be obtained by contacting the Teaching Resource Center. The Galileo Resources Guide is a comprehensive listing of all Galileo educators' resources and how to obtain them. Integrating Galileo Resources Into Your Classroom gives some ideas for classroom activities that use some of those resources.

R	GL	TCK	RR	STS	IL	RTD
**	6–12	*	*	*	*	*

GSFC Education K-8
http://pao.gsfc.nasa.gov/gsfc/educ/k-12/k-8/k-8.htm

This includes a variety of K–8 lessons/activities for space and earth sciences from the Goddard Space Center. Examples of classroom lessons and activities are as follows:

- The first liquid fuel rocket and how it worked.
- Assemble your own Space Shuttle glider, a 1:200-scale model of the U.S. Space Shuttle orbiter.
- Scientific balloons
- Goddard missions of the 1990s
- Mission to Planet Earth (MTPE)—publications and education programs
- Earth science—on-line earth science education information forum
- Earth Observing System (EOS)—education
- TOMS Ozone—difference from climatology
- Total Ozone Mapping (TOMS)—homepage
- Earth view
- Living ocean—teachers' guide
- Global sea surface temperature
- First image of the global biosphere
- World cloud cover pattern
- Tropical Rainfall Measuring Mission (TRMM)—science data and information system
- Hubble Space Telescope first servicing mission
- Astronauts training for Hubble Space Telescope servicing mission

- Revealing secrets of the Big Bang
- WIND laboratory
- The exploration of the earth's magnetosphere
- POLAR laboratory
- Pegasus space launch vehicle
- NASA's scout launch vehicle
- The Delta expendable launch vehicle
- Bright supernova captured in x-ray images

R	GL	TCK	RR	STS	IL	RTD
*	K–8			*	*	

Hands-on-Science
http://dac3.pfrr.alaska.edu/~ddr/ASGP/HANDSON/

Hands-on-Science activities feature Ooze City: creating a complex city with microscopic inhabitants; Auroral Photography: capturing the aurora on film; and Making Aurora: A Classroom Game. You will enjoy looking at this simple and yet interesting site.

R	GL	TCK	RR	STS	IL	RTD
*	K–8			*	*	

Education Planet - e.g. Volcanoes
http://www.educationplanet.com/articles/volcano.html#four

Education Planet is an all-encompassing Web guide for education links and Web-based educational resources. An example is under the subject of volcanoes, where the site has volcano news, volcano lesson plans, specific volcano information, volcano activities and links to resources and suggested readings on volcanoes, for teachers and students alike. The Education Planet site includes a simple search engine with connection to "100,000+" sites for educational resources; a test run with the keyword "weather" yielded 377 Web sites and 152 lesson plans. To access these lesson plans you must register with Lesson Planet, the lesson plan section of Education Planet; however, registration is comparatively easy and is free.

R	GL	TCK	RR	STS	IL	RTD
**	K–12			**	**	

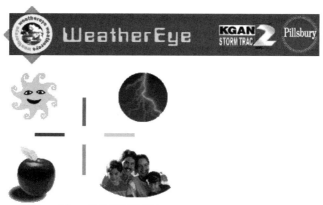

Reprinted with permission of Scott Hall, KGAN-TV.

KGAN WeatherEye Homepage
http://weathereye.kgan.com/

Scott Hall and Roger Evans of KGAN Newschannel 2 in Cedar Rapids, Iowa, feature lesson plans and on-line resources for the study of weather in grades 2–12. The following resources are available:

- Cadet section for grades 2 to 8
- Expert section for grades 6 to 12
- Teachers' lounge lesson plans and resources
- Parents' center fun with your children!

R	GL	TCK	RR	STS	IL	RTD
**	2–12	*	*	*	*	

Education.com TEACHSPACE
http://www.education.com/

Register for membership in this site (free) and you will have access to teaching plans, teaching tips, educational resources and sites for children of all ages. The site is divided into three areas, the largest of which is the teacher's site. This can be searched for lessons and resources by keyword (with an easy-to-use search engine).

R	GL	TCK	RR	STS	IL	RTD
**	K–12	*	*	*	*	*

Reprinted with permission of Northwest Regional Educational Laboratory, Portland, Oregon.

Library in the Sky
http://www.nwrel.org/sky/

The Library in the Sky is for teachers, students, parents, librarians, and the community. It is sponsored by the Northwest Regional Educational Laboratory. Comprehensive educational resources, projects, discussions, collaborations, and standards for K-12 are available in various subject domains: arts, language, mathematics, science, social studies, health, and technology.

Science topics are as follows:

- Astronomy
- Biology
- Botany
- Chemistry
- Earth sciences
- Ecology
- General science
- Geography
- Physics
- Problem solving
- Standards

Each science topic is generally organized into several subtopics (e.g., biology—amphibians, birds, fish, insects, reptiles, and mammals), discussions with experts (e.g., ask an astronaut), lesson plans (e.g., global warming), lists (e.g., careers in biology), references and materials (e.g., construction plans for solar cookers), papers (e.g., understanding our planet through chemistry), periodicals (e.g., *Discover* magazine), projects (e.g., problem-solving activities in physics), and trips (e.g., Smithsonian gem and mineral collection).

R	GL	TCK	RR	STS	IL	RTD
**	K–12	*	*	*	*	*

Source: NASA.

Online From Jupiter
http://quest.arc.nasa.gov/project/jupiter.html

The Online From Jupiter project provides information about the Galileo mission to K–12 teachers.

Options include:

What's New With Online From Jupiter

Background about the spacecraft and its mission

Journal reports from Galileo personnel describing their day-to-day activities and their particular role in the project that will help students understand the diversity of people and skills that are needed for success in a modern science project

Biographical sketches of the men and women of the Galileo project that will help students relate to the project at a human level

An archive of previous question/answer pairs

Feature activities meant especially to stimulate students

Resources for learning, including curriculum materials about Jupiter and Galileo

A Teachers' Lounge that allows discussion among teachers (available through e-mail or the Internet) and includes a registration process that enables like-minded teachers to find one another for possible collaborations

A photo gallery of interesting and relevant images

R	GL	TCK	RR	STS	IL	RTD
*	K–12	*	*	*	*	

Science
http://www.rsf.k12.ca.us/Subjects/Science.html

Science Oceanography Ocean Planet is a traveling exhibition. It features educational resources (lesson plans) as well as images and tours. Topics that are available include:

- The lighthouse
- Weather forecasts
- The weather unit
- Interactive weather browser
- Current weather
- Weather links
- Forecasts

R	GL	TCK	RR	STS	IL	RTD
*	K–12	*	*	*	*	*

Source: NASA.

Spacelink Instructional Materials
http://spacelink.msfc.nasa.gov/Instructional.Materials/.index.html

Or:
**http://spacelink.nasa.gov/Instructional.Materials/Curriculum.Support/
Space.Science/Educator.Guides.and.Activities/.index.html**

NASA provides a variety of downloadable interdisciplinary lesson plans, teacher activity guides, and video resource guides for learning about space for grades K–12. In addition, the site offers a wealth of curriculum materials and activities for the study of aeronautics, different topics in the sciences, and space technology tools. Topics are astronomy, chemistry, electronic resources for educators, environmental science, general science, geology, life sciences, microgravity, physical science, and physics.

R	GL	TCK	RR	STS	IL	RTD
*	*	*	*	*	*	

Teacher-Developed Lesson Plans—University of California Berkeley Space Science
http://cse.ssl.berkeley.edu/euve_epo/Education_curriculum.html/

There are 16 teacher-developed earth and space science lessons that provide classroom demonstrations and activities for grades 4–12. Examples of lessons are solar system, earthquakes, and volcanoes, and there is a lesson template to create your own lesson. Students can conduct research through the Internet.

R	GL	TCK	RR	STS	IL	RTD
*	4–12	*	*	*	*	

Source: Maura Hogan, U.S. Geological Survey.

Teaching in the Learning Web at the USGS
http://www.usgs.gov/education/learnweb/

The U.S. Geological Survey provides earth science lessons for grades 1–12 that aim to increase scientific literacy. These lessons, tested and reviewed by teachers and students, meet the national earth science curriculum standards. Global Change features five classroom activities. Working with Maps includes an interdisciplinary set of materials on mapping for grades 7–12. Both topics include a teacher's guide, while the earth science topic offers pictures and activities about three faults. Other sites are included.

R	GL	TCK	RR	STS	IL	RTD
*	1–12	*	*	*	*	

The Nine Planets
http://seds.lpl.arizona.edu/nineplanets/nineplanets/nineplanets.html

The Nine Planets site provides detailed information about the solar system, graphically represented. Information includes an overview of the history, mythology, and current scientific knowledge of each of the planets and moons in our solar system. Each page has text and images while some have sounds and movies and most provide references to additional related information. This site is mainly for teacher content knowledge. Secondary students may use this site for doing research reports on planets.

R	GL	TCK	RR	STS	IL	RTD
**	K–12	*	*	*		*

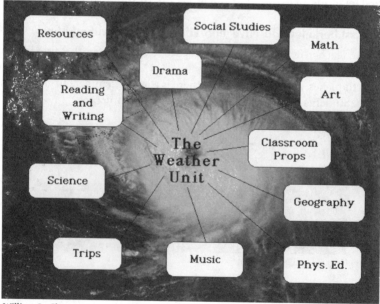

Source: William L. Chapman.

The Weather Unit
http://faldo.atmos.uiuc.edu/WEATHER/weather.html

The Weather Unit develops a multidisciplinary approach. Science lesson plans related to weather for grades K–12 include precipitation, condensation, seasons, and evaporation. Teaching strategies include debate, story, experiment, and games.

R	GL	TCK	RR	STS	IL	RTD
*	K–12	*	*	*	*	

Source: Courtesy of Calvin V. Hamilton.

Views of the Solar System
http://www.hawastsoc.org/solar

Views of the Solar System is an educational tour of the solar system. The table of contents has links to all of the site's various pages including lesson plans and activities. Views of the Solar System contains over 220 Web pages of information and over 950 pictures and animations of the sun, planets, moons, asteroids, comets, and meteoroids found within the solar system. The site also contains lesson activities.

R	GL	TCK	RR	STS	IL	RTD
**	4–12	*	*	*	*	*

Source: National Center for Supercomputing Applications.

Weather Here and There
http://www.ncsa.uiuc.edu/edu/RSE/RSEred/WeatherHome.html

This is an integrated weather unit incorporating interactive, hands-on, collaborative problem-solving lessons and activities for students in grades 4–6. This unit is divided into 6 lessons. The lessons integrate math, science, geography, and language arts in the process of teaching and learning about weather phenomena. Students will become involved in collaborative problem-solving using e-mail as well as through joining projects offered via the Internet. The Global Education Project will help students see the relevance of science by interacting with scientists and other students across the world as they collaborate in the study of weather in their environment.

The first 3 lessons focus on learning basic meteorological concepts about weather elements, how to take measurements using appropriate weather instruments, and recognizing basic weather trends and patterns.

The last 3 lessons focus on studying weather maps and applying the knowledge and experience about weather to anticipate weather trends and patterns in the process of making accurate forecasts. The unit culminates with a weather broadcast of a 24-hour forecast presented by students and focusing on a network of weather stations in the US created by the students.

- Unit directory
- Unit objectives
- Unit outline
- Student pages
- Lesson descriptions and objectives
- Lesson I: characteristics of the earth's atmosphere
- Lesson II: observing the weather

- Lesson III: air affects weather
- Lesson IV: plotting weather on the move
- Lesson V: forecasting the weather
- Lesson VI: broadcasting the weather
- Suggested Internet sites
- Illinois state science goals for learning
- Bibliography

R	GL	TCK	RR	STS	IL	RTD
**	4–6	*	*	*	*	

Reprinted with permission of Corel Corporation.

Weather for Kids
http://www.wxdude.com/

This site provides teachers and parents with Nick's favorite resource materials for kids, teachers and parents to learn more about weather and other sciences. The site's main feature is Nick's Weather Book: Online version. Contents of the book includes:

- Chapter One: Meteorology. Song: "Weather Dude"
- Chapter Two: Precipitation. Song: "What Makes Rain?"
- Chapter Three: Lightning and Thunder. Song: "Thunderstorms"
- Chapter Four: Clouds. Song: "Cloud Cover"
- Chapter Five: Snow. Song: "Wonderland"
- Chapter Six: The Sun. Song: "You're There in the Sky for Me"
- Chapter Seven: Air Pressure. Song: "That's the Way Winds Blow"
- Chapter Eight: The Seasons. Song: "Circle of Our Four Seasons"
- Chapter Nine: Weather Forecasting. Song: "Tomorrow's Weather Here Today"
- Chapter Ten: The Water Cycle. Song: "A Tiny Drop of Water"

Other links available on the site are:

- Meteorology A to Z
- Forecasts, Maps & Records
- Weather Songs
- Stuff for Teachers/Parents
- Stuff for Kids
- Atmospheric Art
- Weather Gift Ideas
- Favorite Weather Books for Kids, Parents & Teachers
- Weather Questions & Quizzes
- Weather Headlines

R	GL	TCK	RR	STS	IL	RTD
**	K–12	*	*	*	*	

Source: © University of Michigan and NASA.

Windows to the Universe
http://www.windows.ucar.edu

NASA has sponsored a dynamic presentation of earth and space sciences. Choose beginner, intermediate, or advanced interest levels.

R	GL	TCK	RR	STS	IL	RTD
*	6–12	*	*	*		

LIFE SCIENCE

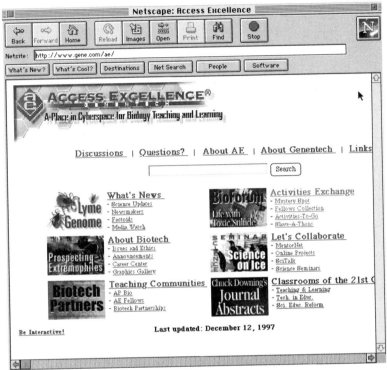

Source: Access Excellence and Genentech, Inc.

Access Excellence
www.accessexcellence.org

This site consists of resources for biology teaching and learning. Resources include science updates, issues, and ethics about biotechnology, links to teaching communities, activities exchange, collaboration, and journal abstracts. High school biology teachers are connected with scientists, scientific information, and each other through the on-line network, Access Excellence. This national education program is sponsored by Genentech, Inc.

R	GL	TCK	RR	STS	IL	RTD
**	9–12	*	*	*		*

Africanized Honey Bees on the Move Homepage
http://ag.arizona.edu/pubs/insects/ahb/ahbhome.html

Roberta Gibson at the University of Arizona features 30 lesson plans about honey bees and bee safety issues. These lessons are organized by grade clusters. The lesson plans are also integrated with information sheets that provide theoretical information for the teacher. Activity sheets are available for students.

R	GL	TCK	RR	STS	IL	RTD
**	K–12	*	*		*	*

Reprinted with permission of Kathleen M. Fisher, San Diego State University.

Biology Lessons at SDSU
http://www.biologylessons.sdsu.edu/index.html

Students at San Diego State University offer lesson plans in a variety of topics in biology for use in elementary school classrooms. This site presents lessons in molecules and cells and provides students and teachers with knowledge mapping and SemNet Web links to major biological content.

R	GL	TCK	RR	STS	IL	RTD
**	K–8				*	

Mini-Unit Topic: Insects
http://www.ed.uiuc.edu/YLP/Units/Mini_Units/94-95/Griffin.Insects

A preservice teacher has prepared an introductory unit to the world of insects for grades 2 and 3. Suggested extension ideas are listed at the end of each lesson for those interested in developing this unit into an actual unit to be covered over an extended period of time (3 to 4 weeks). Some of the ideas for the art lesson are borrowed from the first 8-week cooperating teacher who taught an entire unit on insects. But most of the ideas for the other lessons are prepared by the preservice teacher. In addition to the four lessons required for this assignment, the preservice teacher has also made an entirely different lesson (partly based on one of the mini-unit lessons) for a 5th-grade class based on the second 8-week placement. This lesson may also be used in 2nd- or 3rd-grade classes, but the preservice teacher strongly suggests postponing the lesson until 4th or 5th grade due to its rather complex nature.

R	GL	TCK	RR	STS	IL	RTD
*	2–3					

Source: NASA Goddard Space Flight Center.

SeaWiFS Project
http://seawifs.gsfc.nasa.gov/SEAWIFS.html

NASA's Goddard Space Flight Center provides a teacher's guide featuring on-line activities with answers for high school students to study ocean color from space. The topics include life in the ocean, the ocean isn't just blue, phytoplankton, the earth, and carbon. Other resources include announcements, people collaboration, software documentation, technical reports, spacecraft information, receiving stations, mission operations, data sets images, and calibration validation.

R	GL	TCK	RR	STS	IL	RTD
*	11–12	*	*	*		*

© 1998 The Yuckiest Site on the Internet, www.yucky.com.

The Yuckiest Site on the Internet
http://yucky.kids.discovery.com

The Yuckiest Site on the Internet features information about health, worms, and cockroaches. To find a variety of resources, click on Your Gross & Cool Body, Wendell's Worm World, Ask Wendell, or Wendell's Yucky Bug World.

R	GL	TCK	RR	STS	IL	RTD
*	K–6	*				

Reprinted with permission of Kimberlye P. Joyce, University of Richmond.

Whales
http://curry.edschool.Virginia.EDU/go/Whales/

Whales: A Thematic Web Unit is an integrated, interactive curriculum unit that can be used by teachers, students, and parents. The table of contents contains cooperative lesson plans (i.e., Teacher Guides from Sea World), teacher resources, interactive student activities, and projects with links to related sites.

R	GL	TCK	RR	STS	IL	RTD
**	4–8	*	*	*	*	*

Source: Wildlife Discovery Program and Houston Independent School Disctrict.

Wildlife Discovery
http://www.rice.edu/armadillo/Schools/Hisdzoo/

The Houston Zoo and the Houston Independent School District present lessons for teaching about endangered animals for grades 3–6. Click on activity sheets that you can use at any zoo. The site also includes an on-line quiz about wild animals, a bilingual glossary of zoo terms, a list of frequently asked questions (FAQs), and facts about wildlife. Some of the information files must be downloaded.

R	GL	TCK	RR	STS	IL	RTD
**	3–6	*	*	*	*	*

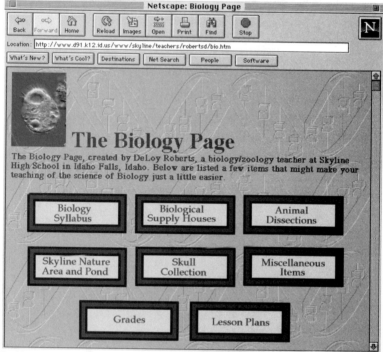

Reprinted with permission of DeLoy Roberts, Skyline High School.

The Biology Page
http://www.d91.k12.id.us/www/skyline/teachers/robertsd/bio.htm

The Biology Page is created by DeLoy Roberts, a biology/zoology teacher at Skyline High School in Idaho Falls, Idaho. He provides a syllabus for biology, dissections of animals, the collection of skulls, and a list of biological supply houses.

R	GL	TCK	RR	STS	IL	RTD
**	11–12	*	*	*		

Source: David Wighton, Community Learning Network.

Brain/Nervous System Theme Page
http://www.cln.org/themes/brain.html

This site provides links to resources related to the study of the brain and nervous system. Students as well as teachers will find curricular resources and materials to help them learn about the brain and nervous system. Also, this site is linked to instructional materials (lesson plans) such as Neuroscience for Kids and Overview of the Brain.

R	GL	TCK	RR	STS	IL	RTD
**	K–12	*	*	*	*	*

Endangered Species Theme Page
http://www.cln.org/themes/endangered.html

This site has links to information and content related to the study of endangered species. Lesson plans are also available for teachers and students. Interesting sites include For Kids Only: World Wildlife Fund Canada; Here Today, Gone Tomorrow?; and Investigating Endangered Species in the Classroom.

R	GL	TCK	RR	STS	IL	RTD
**	K–12	*	*	*	*	*

Photo reprinted with permission of Keith P. Turner, © 1996.

From the Ground Up
http://www.gatewest.net/~green/from/index.html

This site provides a teacher's guide that consists of lessons such as food, agriculture, and sustainable development: history of agriculture and description of sustainable development, soil, agriculture and chemicals, the real cost of food, and everything is connected. Lessons, background essays, and worksheets are available for downloading.

R	GL	TCK	RR	STS	IL	RTD
**	10–12	*	*	*	*	

Genetics/Biotechnology Theme Page
http://www.cln.org/themes/genetics.html

This site has links to information and content related to the study of genetics and biotechnology. Lesson plans are also available for teachers and students. Interesting sites include Genetics Lesson Plan Ideas, Genetics and Public Issues, and DNA Learning Center.

R	GL	TCK	RR	STS	IL	RTD
**	10–12	*	*	*	*	*

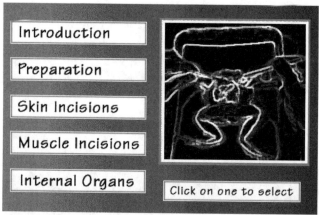

Reprinted with permission. Copyright 1994, Mable Kinzie.

Interactive Frog Dissection
http://curry.edschool.virginia.edu/go/frog/

This site teaches students how to dissect a frog and provides an understanding of the anatomy of frogs and vertebrate animals in general, including humans. Still and motion visuals of preserved frogs are shown.

R	GL	TCK	RR	STS	IL	RTD
**	10–12	*				*

Fetal Pig Dissection Page
http://hyperion.advanced.org/12014/links.html

This site provides numerous links to instruction materials on dissection. Sites include Science Kit's Homepage, the Dissection Lab, and Classification Lab.

R	GL	TCK	RR	STS	IL	RTD
**	10–12	*				*

Reprinted with permission of Southwest Educational Development Laboratory.

Integrating Mathematics, Science, and Language
http://www.sedl.org/scimath/pasopartners/

This site offers a series of multidisciplinary units. Each unit consists of an overview and background information for the teacher and lessons and links to associated Web sites. Units include kindergarten (Five Senses, Spiders, Dinosaurs); grade 1 (Plants and Seeds, the Human Body, Good Health); grade 2 (Oceans, Weather, Sun and Stars); grade 3 (Matter, Sound, Simple Machines).

R	GL	TCK	RR	STS	IL	RTD
**	K–3	*	*	*	*	*

Reprinted with permission of Janet W. Azbell, IBM Education, ISU.

IBM Global Industries Education Homepage
http://www-1.ibm.com/industries/education/

In this site IBM provides a set of Internet lesson plans for all grade levels and topics, including a variety of science lesson plans. These can be downloaded after registration (free).

R	GL	TCK	RR	STS	IL	RTD
**	K–12	*	*	*	*	*

Oceanography
http://www.cln.org/themes/oceanography.html

This site has links to information and content related to the study of oceanography. Lesson plans are also available for teachers and students. Links such as the El Niño site, the Whales Theme Page, Elementary Lesson Plans, Resources on Oceans, Whales and Sea Life, and Sea World at Busch Gardens are available.

R	GL	TCK	RR	STS	IL	RTD
**	K–12	*	*	*	*	*

Respiratory System Theme Page
http://www.cln.org/themes/respiratory.html

This site has links to the information and content related to the study of the respiratory system. Lesson plans are also available for teachers and students. Links such as the American Lung Association, Canadian Lung Association Resources, Grade 5 Life Science (Body Systems—Respiratory, Circulatory, Sensory), and Science Role Plays are available.

R	GL	TCK	RR	STS	IL	RTD
**	K–12	*	*	*	*	*

PHYSICAL SCIENCES

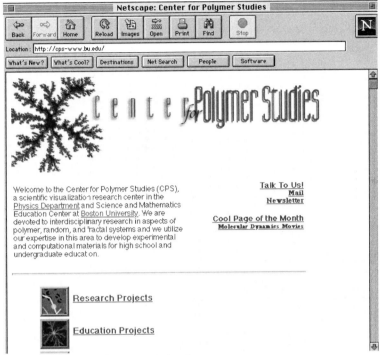

Source: Center for Polymer Studies, Boston University.

Center for Polymer Studies
http://cps-www.bu.edu/

This scientific visualization research center develops experimental and computational materials for high school science education. Information resource links include Research Projects, Education Projects, Patterns in Nature Student Activity Guides, Fractals in Science Simulations (Java-Powered), the Dance of Chance Science Museum Exhibit, and Molecular Dynamics Simulations.

R	GL	TCK	RR	RD	IL	RTD
**	11–12	*	*	*		

Chemistry Teaching Resources
http://www.brocku.ca/library/research/chem/teach.htm

This site lists dozens of on-line chemistry resource pages including sites for obtaining lesson plans and other educational materials. Some of the sites listed include:

- Analytical Chemistry Teaching Resources (Umea Univ.)
- ChemCAI (Steve Lower, Simon Fraser University)

- Chemistry Classes Online (Univ. South Carolina ELP Project)
- CHEMystery—Virtual Chemistry Textbook
- General Chemistry Online (Fred Senese, Frostberg State University)
- General Chemistry Virtual Textbook (Michael Blaber, Florida State University)
- Internet Site for Freshman Chemistry (Univ. Waterloo)

R	GL	TCK	RR	STS	IL	RTD
*	10–12	*	*	*	*	

Reprinted with permission of the California Energy Commission.

Energy Quest Homepage
http://www.energy.ca.gov/education/

This site contains activities and projects on alternative sources of energy, fuel vehicles, and energy safety.

R	GL	TCK	RR	STS	IL	RTD
*	K–12	*	*	*	*	

Source: The Pan-Educational Institute.

PEI Homepage
http://www.pei.edu/

This site contains resources for teachers including lesson plans, interactive lessons, and chemical safety information. Many links are available.

R	GL	TCK	RR	STS	IL	RTD
**	K–12	*	*	*	*	*

Physical Science Lessons
http://www.eecs.umich.edu/mathscience/funexperiments/agesubject/physicalsciences.html

There are more than 100 physical science lessons for early elementary, later elementary, middle school, and high school students. Examples of lessons are:

- How do you make paper?
- How does soap work?
- The pizza box solar oven
- What is macaroni made of?
- What is thunder?
- Why does a steel nail sink while a steel boat floats?

- Playing with polymers
- Air bags and collisions: How do air bags prevent automobile injuries?
- Air pressure: What is air pressure, and how can it be measured?
- What makes the world turn around?
- Microwave ovens: What is the science behind microwave cooking?
- Slinky physics: How do toys work?
- What is infrared light, and how does it work?

R	GL	TCK	RR	STS	IL	RTD
**	K–12	*	*	*	*	

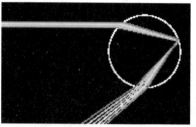 

Source: The Geometry Center, University of Minnesota.

Rainbow Lab
http://www.geom.umn.edu/education/calc-init/rainbow/

This lab helps to answer these and other questions: How are rainbows formed? Why do they occur only when the sun is behind the observer? The outline for this site is as follows:

- Objectives of the lab
- How does light travel?
- Reflection
- Refraction
- Rainbows: exploration
- Rainbows: analysis
- Conclusion

R	GL	TCK	RR	STS	IL	RTD
**	K–12	*	*	*	*	

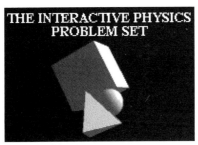

Source: © Regents of the University of California.

The Interactive Physics Problem Set
http://socrates.berkeley.edu:7521/projects/IPPS/Contents.html

The site consists of almost 100 practice problems for physics students with solutions and interactive experiments and Moving Pictures Experts Group (mpeg) movies.

R	GL	TCK	RR	STS	IL	RTD
*	11–12	*	*	*	*	

Reprinted with permission of Kyle Yamnitz, University of Missouri.

The Lesson Plans Page
http://www.lessonplanspage.com/Science.htm

This site provides personal assignments and lesson plans on topics such as clouds and magnets. This page currently consists of links to lesson plan pages that are very helpful for anyone in education.

R	GL	TCK	RR	STS	IL	RTD
**	K–12	*	*	*	*	

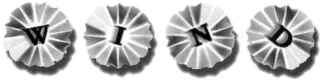

Reprinted with permission of The Franklin Institute Science Museum.

Wind Our Fierce Friend
http://sln.fi.edu/tfi/units/energy/wind.html

The Franklin Institute Museum of Science presents an interactive collaborative unit that investigates wind energy. The site contains lessons and activities that include student contributions from on-line schools. Content includes Blustery Beginnings, Investigating Wind Energy, Current Creations, and What Next?

R	GL	TCK	RR	STS	IL	RTD
*	4–6	*	*	*	*	

GENERAL SCIENCE

Activity Search
http://www.hmco.com/hmco/school/search/activity2.html

Houghton Mifflin features a curriculum database where K–8 teachers can search for science lesson plans and activities by theme and grade level. Activities include Life Cycle of the Pacific Salmon, Catastrophe versus Accident—You Decide, Let's Make Waves, and Wind Direction.

R	GL	TCK	RR	STS	IL	RTD
*	K–8				*	

Source: W. J. Beaty.

Amateur Science
http://www.eskimo.com/~billb/amasci.html

Amateur Science contains hundreds of science activities, experiments, and projects. Visit Bill Beaty's collection of science projects and the collection of science projects from various Web sites. Some of the sites include:

■ Science Fair Stuff

■ American Science Books

■ Science Education Discussion Lists

■ Science Education Stores

■ Science and Surplus Suppliers

■ Static Electricity Project Page

■ Electronic Hobbyist Page

■ Patents

■ Bill B's Hobby Projects

R	GL	TCK	RR	STS	IL	RTD
**	4–12	*	*	*	*	*

General Science
http://www.nwrel.org/sky/index.asp

Note: Click on the Science link

General Science is a library in the sky for teachers, students, and parents. Main site headings available are Discussions, Lesson Plans, Lists, Materials, Multimedia, Papers, and Periodicals.

R	GL	TCK	RR	STS	IL	RTD
**	K–12	*	*	*	*	*

ERIC Online
http://ericir.syr.edu/cgi-bin/lessons.cgi/Science

This site includes lesson plans and hands-on experiments for all levels of students, including Backpack Science, Bubble-ology and Ice Cream in a Bag.

R	GL	TCK	RR	STS	IL	RTD
**	K–12	*	*	*	*	*

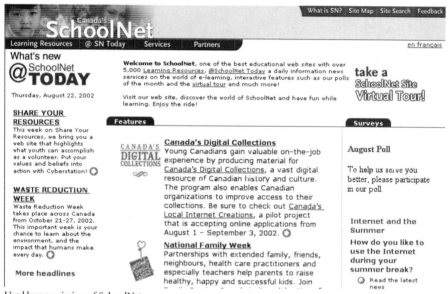

Used by permission of SchoolNet.

SCHOOLNET.CA
http://www.schoolnet.ca

This Canadian government site has learning resources for all aspects of science under the general headings: Biology, Biotechnology, Chemistry, Earth Science and Geology, Engineering, Physics, Resource Sciences, and Space and Astronomy. Links to other education resources and governmental agencies, museums, etc. are also included.

R	GL	TCK	RR	STS	IL	RTD
**	K–12	*	*	**	*	*

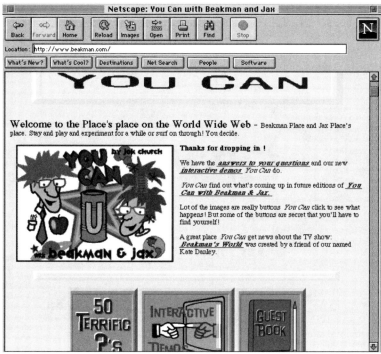

Source: Jok Church.

You Can with Beakman and Jax
http://www.beakman.com/

Jok R. Church's television show Beakman's World can be used for science lessons. Click on 50 Terrific Questions, where you will find a range of questions and answers with accompanying science activities. Questions include: How does a lever make you stronger? Why do I hear weird sounds at night? How does yeast make bread rise? and What is thunder made out of?

R	GL	TCK	RR	STS	IL	RTD
**	K–8	*	*	*	*	*

ELEMENTARY SCIENCE

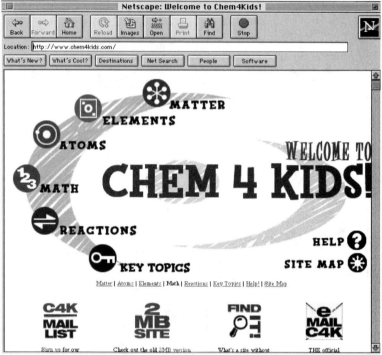

Source: Andrew S. Rader, Rader New Media.

CHEM 4 KIDS
http://www.chem4kids.com/

Chem 4 Kids teaches the basics of chemistry to children ages 5 to 11 in a fun way. The content outline includes matter, elements, atoms, and reactions.

R	GL	TCK	RR	STS	IL	RTD
*	K–8	*	*			

Reprinted with permission of the National Science Teachers Association.

Dragonfly
http://www.muohio.edu/Dragonfly/index.htmlx

Dragonfly Web pages are for investigators of all ages. These pages go with Dragonfly magazine, but you do not need the magazine to have fun here. Right now the Dragonfly is exploring science and nature.

R	GL	TCK	RR	STS	IL	RTD
**	K–8	*	*	*		*

Used with permission of the Internet Public Library, University of Michigan.

Dr. Internet
http://ipl.sils.umich.edu/youth/DrInternet/

Dr. Internet is for children to explore science fun and facts on the Web. The content outline for this site is as follows:

- Dr. Internet's Science Projects
- Explore the Internet with Dr. I.
- Science Fair Project Resource Guide

R	GL	TCK	RR	STS	IL	RTD
*	K–8	*	*	*	*	

Helping Your Child Learn Science
http://www.ed.gov/pubs/parents/Science/index.html

This site has suggestions for parents to interest their children in science and includes basics about science and activities for children, including bubbles, plants, crystals, bugs, and soap powder.

R	GL	TCK	RR	STS	IL	RTD
*	K–8			*	*	

KIDS AS GLOBAL SCIENTISTS
http://groundhog.sprl.umich.edu/kgs01.html

Kids as Global Scientists is an inquiry-based educational program designed to enable elementary to middle school children to learn about the atmosphere, weather and the environment.

R	GL	TCK	RR	STS	IL	RTD
*	6–8			*	*	

Science Activities Manual K–8
http://www.utm.edu/departments/ed/cece/SAMK8.shtml

The Science Activities Manual (SAM) supports the K–8 Tennessee Science Curriculum Framework. SAM addresses content with a hands-on approach and also incorporates the skills necessary to raise the activity to a higher cognition level. This emphasis on both the physical and mental aspects of teaching and learning science is also called "touch science." The major motivation is to employ instructional strategies that bring the students physically and mentally into touch with the science they are studying.

R	GL	TCK	RR	STS	IL	RTD
*	K–8	*	*	*		*

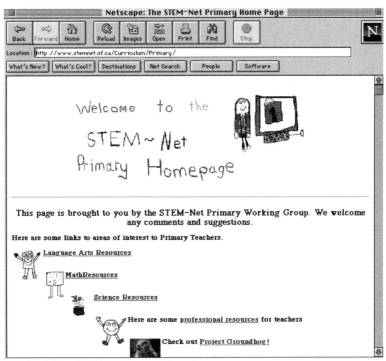

Source: Wendy M. King, STEM-Net Program Council.

STEM~Net Primary Homepage
http://www.stemnet.nf.ca/curriculum/science.shtml

STEM~Net Primary Homepage provides a thematic unit on penguins. It features a variety of cross-curricular lesson plans for students in the primary grades.

R	GL	TCK	RR	STS	IL	RTD
*	K–8	*	*			

The Year Long Project 1996–1997
http://www.ed.uiuc.edu/ylp/96–97/

University of Illinois at Champaign-Urbana and local elementary school teachers provide 11 cross-curricular science mini-units developed by student teachers and 8 cross-curricular science mini-units contributed by assistant teachers.

R	GL	TCK	RR	STS	IL	RTD
**	K–8	*	*	*	*	*

Reprinted with permission of the Science Museum of Minnesota.

Thinking Fountain
http://www.smm.org/sln/

The Science Museum of Minnesota provides an unusual collection of science activities on a site called the Thinking Fountain. An interactive graphic invites students, teachers, and other visitors to dive directly into the activities. The Thinking Fountain offers several additional ways to find an idea of interest, including going directly to an alphabetical listing, exploring by thematic topic, or typing in a word to search. Visitors to the site are encouraged to submit their own activities and questions to add to this wellspring of ideas.

R	GL	TCK	RR	STS	IL	RTD
**	K–6	*	*	*	*	

SECONDARY SCIENCE

Ask a Scientist
http://www.trabuco.org/

This site provides on-line homework help in all of the sciences. This Web site also provides a link to the NASA homepage.

R	GL	TCK	RR	STS	IL	RTD
**	K–12			*		

Geometry in Space Project
http://www.cs.bsu.edu/homepages/dathomas/SpaceGrant/

This site is part of NASA's Web education project and uses space and space travel as a medium for geometry and other problems. Students will calculate spacecraft trajectories and plot landing sites among other activities. The applied approach integrates basic science and reasoning skills with the imagination-grabbing excitement of space travel.

R	GL	TCK	RR	STS	IL	RTD
**	7–12	*	*	*		

K–12 SCIENCE

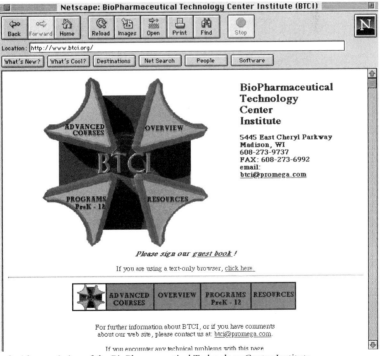

Reprinted with permission of the BioPharmaceutical Technology Center Institute.

BioPharmaceutical Technology Center Institute
http://www.btci.org/

This site focuses on biotechnology training and education. Programs range from introductory lab activities for kindergartners to grade level courses for students, faculty, and industry scientists. A list of useful biotechnology resource books, articles, pamphlets, Web sites, and much more is included.

R	GL	TCK	RR	STS	IL	RTD
*	K–12	*	*	*		

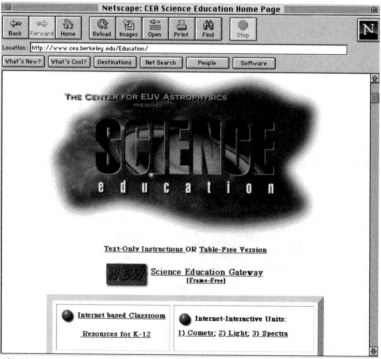

Reprinted with permission of the University of California, Berkeley.

CEA Science Education Home Page
http://ssl.berkeley.edu/euve/

This site contains Internet-interactive units on comets, light, and spectra. Lesson plans and activities are designed by K–12 science teachers and students. Other subject indexes included in this Web site are Science Information Infrastructure (SII), Talk of the Town: A Discussion Forum Generator for Education, and the EUVE Slideshow.

R	GL	TCK	RR	STS	IL	RTD
**	K–12	*	*	*	*	*

Educational Hotlist
http://sln.fi.edu/tfi/hotlists/hotlists.html

Educational Hotlist is divided into three main groups (general topics, science, and teacher resources) and includes lesson ideas and projects. Some of the topics include:

- Atomic Structure
- Chemistry 101
- Forensic Science Web Site
- Einstein Revealed
- Chemical of the Week
- Chemicool-Periodic Table
- Complexity and Organic Development
- NIST Chemical Web Book
- Electromagnetic Spectrum

R	GL	TCK	RR	STS	IL	RTD
**	K–12	*	*	*	*	*

General Links to Lesson Plans
http://tikkun.ed.asu.edu/coe/links/lessons.html

For K–12.

- Lesson Plans from ASKEric at Syracuse University (Gopher)
- Elementary Science Lesson Plans (Gopher)
- Holocaust Curriculum Plans (Gopher)
- Lesson Plans in All Areas (Gopher)
- Lesson Plans from ERIC-AE at Catholic University of America (Gopher)
- Lesson Plans in Environmental Education (Gopher)
- Lesson Plans in Science and Math from the HUB (Gopher)
- Science Lesson Plans from Bolt, Beranek, and Newman (Gopher)
- Lesson Plans from Teacher Talk Forum (WWW)
- Lesson Plans and Projects from SAMI (WWW)
- Lesson Plans and Resources for K-6 (WWW)
- Classroom Resources for Environmental Education (WWW)

R	GL	TCK	RR	STS	IL	RTD
**	K–12	*	*	*	*	

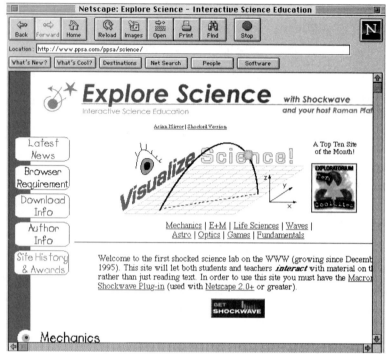

Reprinted with permission of the University of Michigan.

Interactive Science Education
http://www.explorescience.com

Topics included are on-line experiments in mechanics, density, genetics, and plasma, including a frictionless inclined plane with sliding object. Other subject headings include Mechanics, E+M, Life Sciences, Waves, Astro, Optics, Games, and Fundamentals.

R	GL	TCK	RR	STS	IL	RTD
*	K–12	*	*	*	*	*

Internet School Library Media Center
http://falcon.jmu.edu/~ramseyil/

This media center offers a comprehensive guide to children's and young adult literature, curriculum units, lesson plans, and resources in subject disciplines such as history, math, science, and social science.

R	GL	TCK	RR	STS	IL	RTD
*	K–12	*	*	*	*	

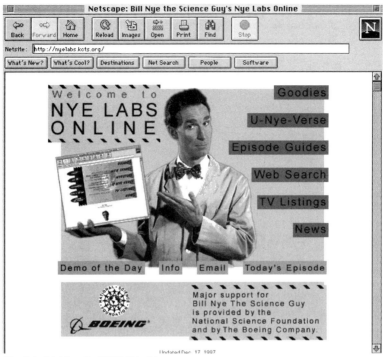

Source: Nye Labs Multimedia, KCTS Television.

Nye's Lab Online
http://www.billnye.com/

Behind Bill's spinning head you will find his daily episode plus links to quality science education resources.

R	GL	TCK	RR	STS	IL	RTD
*	K–12	*	*	*		

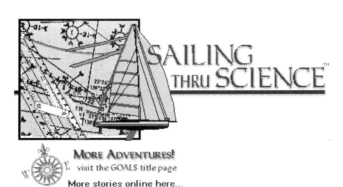

Source: John Omar, GOALS (Global Online Adventure Learning Site).

GOALS: Global Online Adventure Learning Site—Sailing Through Science
http://www.goals.com/ClassRm/SailSci/SailSciF.htm

It contains exercises and projects directly related to the scientific principles involved in circumnavigating the world. This site will help you understand global navigation, communication, and living at sea.

R	GL	TCK	RR	STS	IL	RTD
*	K–12	*	*	*		

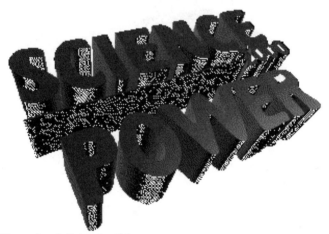

Source: Todd Hoover, Loyola University, Chicago.

Science Power
http://www.luc.edu/schools/education/science.htm

Science Power has links to lesson plans and activities on natural science, earth science, astronomy and space, and Web sites. This is a great resource page for teachers.

R	GL	TCK	RR	STS	IL	RTD
**	K–12	*	*	*	*	*

Columbia University

Summer Science Research Program

Reprinted with permission of Jay Dubner, Columbia University.

Summer Research Program for Science Teachers
http://www.scienceteacherprogram.org/

Summer Research Program for NYC Secondary School Science Teachers homepage contains laboratory research lesson plans developed by the participating teachers. Lesson plan topics include the Pressure-Volume Relationship in Gases (Boyle's Law), Vitamin C and protein analysis, and How is a tokamak used to produce controlled nuclear fusion?

R	GL	TCK	RR	STS	IL	RTD
**	K–12	*	*	*	*	

Teacher Tool Box
http://www.trc.org/

Teacher Tool Box links to sites of interest to K–12 teachers and contains a searchable index where you can look for lesson plans or topics of your interest. There are quicklinks to several sites including MapQuest, Birdfoot's Grandpa, and Flea News.

R	GL	TCK	RR	STS	IL	RTD
**	K–12	*	*	*	*	*

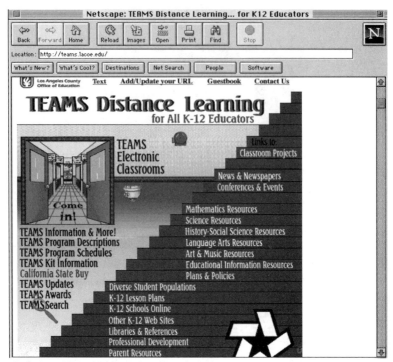

Source: Gayle Perry, TEAMS Distance Learning.

TEAMS Distance Learning for All K–12 Educators
http://teams.lacoe.edu/

Telecommunication Education Advance for Mathematics and Science (TEAMS) distance learning, maintained by the Los Angeles County Office of Education (LACOE), features a variety of lessons, on-line classroom projects, and resources. Some of the interesting lesson plan sites listed are Air Quality Lesson Plans, Barbara's Lesson Plans in Science, and Biology Lessons for Prospective and Practicing Teachers.

R	GL	TCK	RR	STS	IL	RTD
**	K–12	*	*	*	*	*

Reprinted with permission of MedSci Network.

The MAD Scientist Network
http://www.madsci.org/

The MAD Scientist Network—the laboratory that never sleeps—is a collective cranium of scientists from around the world fielding questions in different areas of science. Take a few moments to fill out the on-line question form if you need a question answered. You may also become a member of this Network. Subject headings include:

- ■ *New* MadSci
- ■ Circumnavigator
- ■ Recently Answered Questions
- ■ The MadSci Archives
- ■ Search Our Site
- ■ Ask a Question
- ■ Check a Question's Status
- ■ Join Our Efforts!

R	GL	TCK	RR	STS	IL	RTD
**	K–12	*	*	*		*

Whelmers Home Page
http://www.mcrel.org/whelmers/

Activities on this site correspond with National Science Education standards. Some examples of activities are provided in this homepage. Information is provided in this site to order two volumes consisting of complete K–12 lesson plans. Some of the lesson plans available include Falling Test Tubes, Density Balloon, Energy Transfer, and Potato Float.

R	GL	TCK	RR	STS	IL	RTD
*	K–12	*	*	*	*	

SCIENCE, TECHNOLOGY, AND SOCIETY CONNECTIONS

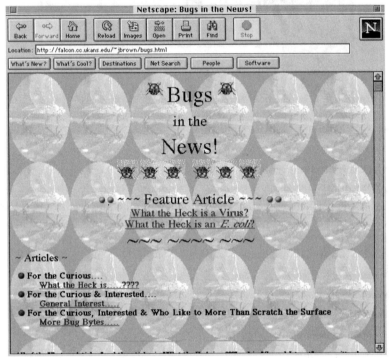

Reprinted with permission of the University of Kansas.

Bugs in the News
http://people.ku.edu/~jbrown/bugs.html

A science professor offers scientific news and knowledge to information seekers in understandable, interesting language. As the title of the page implies, many of the science lessons here are inspired by yesterday's headlines. Two of the featured articles in this site are What the Heck is a Virus? and What the Heck is an E. coli?

R	GL	TCK	RR	STS	IL	RTD
*	9–12	*	*	*		

CyberSchoolBus
http://www.un.org/Pubs/CyberSchoolBus/

CyberSchoolBus, an interactive educational service produced by the United Nations features lesson plans and activities on world issues, photos, competitions, and education resources. Some of the popular topics in this site include global trends, country at a glance, and a science puzzle.

R	GL	TCK	RR	STS	IL	RTD
*	K–12	*	*	*	*	*

Source: CyberSchoolBus, produced by the United Nations.

Global Learning On-Line Homepage
http://giraffe.rmplc.co.uk/eduweb/sites/rmext05/glo/

This site is for anyone interested in finding out or teaching about global issues. The site provides activities and information to get you thinking about global issues and to share good and bad experiences using the Internet as a resource for global education, particularly in school.

R	GL	TCK	RR	STS	IL	RTD
*	K–12	*	*	*	*	

Reprinted with permission of Keep America Beautiful.

Keep America Beautiful Homepage
http://www.kab.org/

This site provides educational information on solid waste management (recycling, composting, waste-to-energy, sanitary landfilling) and litter prevention and offers free lesson plans and other publications on-line. Lesson plans available in this site include Waste: A Hidden Resource, Waste in Place, and Dirt Dessert!

R	GL	TCK	RR	STS	IL	RTD
*	K–12	*	*	*	*	

Liberty-Eylau's Teacher Lesson Plans Area
http://www.lehman.cuny.edu/education/center/DDE/general_lessons.htm

This site provides a variety of WWW links to Web sites that contain science lesson plans for teachers. Some of the sites listed include:

- ERIC Science Lessons
- Big Sky Science Lesson
- More Science Lessons from Doctor Sharp
- ERIC Technology Lessons
- Computer Skills Lesson Plans from North Carolina's Department of Public Instruction
- HTML Guides and Resources
- Teaching Computer Technology
- Investigating Endangered Species in the Classroom
- Programming by Ainsworth Lesson

R	GL	TCK	RR	STS	IL	RTD
**	K–12	*	*	*	*	

Reprinted with permission of Julie Chapin, National Network for Science & Technology.

National Network for Science & Technology
http://www.ets.uidaho.edu/4-H/nnst/

This WWW site is for a youth development professional, a volunteer leader, or anyone looking for hands-on science and technology activities, science education research, or upcoming training and conferences. Resources fall within the scientific method and/or the exploratory learning model. Many of the resources will require adaptation to the nonformal setting.

R	GL	TCK	RR	STS	IL	RTD
**	K–12	*	*	*	*	

NSTW '97,'98-Teaching Activities
http://www.nsf.gov/od/lpa/nstw/teach/start.htm

What's NSTW? How are bridges built over a body of water? Why is the sky blue? Why do ships float but rocks sink? What do earthworms eat? Where do stars come from? Will dinosaurs ever reappear? Is there life similar to earth's on other planets? These questions and thousands of others like them are from children who possess an endless sense of wonder about the world around them and how it works.

The National Science Foundation (NSF) believes that it is important to nurture the natural interests of children and the child in all of us about the wonders of science and technology. That's one of the reasons that more than a decade ago NSF started National Science and Technology Week (NSTW), celebrated at the end of April.

There are two broad components to NSTW: First, NSTW is a series of nationwide special events. The events range from family science nights to science and technology fairs to open houses to hands-on science and technology demonstrations sponsored by NSF and hundreds of community organizations, state agencies, museums, science centers, local businesses, national corporations, libraries, arboretums, planetariums, and zoos.

The second component is hands-on teaching activities that are developed and distributed free of charge to participating organizations. The materials are designed to stimulate both children's imaginations and their understanding of science and technology. By using these materials as instructional exercises, informal and formal science educators teach children how to observe real-world phenomena, analyze variables, draw conclusions, and evaluate findings.

Both the special events and teaching materials have one simple objective: heighten the awareness of children—and their parents and educators!—to the important role played by science and technology in everyday living.

R	GL	TCK	RR	STS	IL	RTD
**	K–12	*	*	*	*	**

PBA Home Page
http://www.plasticbag.com/

This site offers free environmental lesson plans for teachers on the 3 R's: reduce, reuse, and recycle. On-line activities for students dovetail with an activity poster. The lesson plans include Don't Let a Good Thing Go to Waste and An Ounce of Prevention.

R	GL	TCK	RR	STS	IL	RTD
**	K–12	*	*	*	*	*

Reprinted with permission of the Plastic Bag Information Clearinghouse.

Reduce, Reuse, Recycle, Revise, Respond
http://www.ncsu.edu/sciencejunction/terminal/imse/lowres/3/project.htm

Fisher Grade School's 5 Rs learning project is directed at improving grade 6 students' knowledge in environmental science and math as well as their attitudes and behaviors. Students are asked to explore questions related to the 5 Rs. Students examine: What is trash? How much trash do they produce as individuals? as families? as a school? How could they reduce the amount of trash they generate? What does their trash consist of? What does it mean to recycle? Does FGS have a recycling program? How could it be improved? What can they do to promote recycling at school? How does the village of Fisher dispose of its trash? How much trash do residents create? How does Fisher promote recycling? What are some concerns of the businesses and residents of the community?

R	GL	TCK	RR	STS	IL	RTD
*	6–12	*	*	*	*	*

The Living Curriculum Archive
http://204.189.12.10/ed/cur/liv/ind/

The Archive contains lesson plans and unit descriptions with examples of student work in areas such as ecology, writing, math, and social science. Science topics include:

- Birds of a Feather by Jessica Morton, Mendocino Grammar School
- Flight: The Confluence of Dreams and Technology by Claire Skilton and Deena Zarlin, Mendocino Grammar School
- Science Mastery Units by Robert Miller, Mendocino High School
- Earthquakes by David Gross, Mendocino Middle School
- The Study of Local Ecology by Linda Leyva, Mendocino Middle School
- Salmon by Larry White, Mendocino Grammar School

R	GL	TCK	RR	STS	IL	RTD
*	K–12	*	*	*	*	

THE **Why?** FILES™

SCIENCE BEHIND THE NEWS

Archives   The Why Files in Education   Search

In depth:

Invasive Species
10 least wanted
[8 Aug 2002]

As Maryland prepares to kill the nasty snakehead fish, what about the larger problem of invasive species? What's damaging our oceans, wetlands and uplands? Meet the most unwanted!

In brief:

Ultimate Fat Fighter
No enzyme - no fat!
[15 Aug 2002]

Mice lacking the enzyme SCD-1 can eat all they want - and not get fat. Gobble, gobble. Just imagine the possibilities...

In the news:

West Nile virus spread
Another emerging infection

Drought in All 50 States
What you gonna drink?

Yet Another Corpse Flower
Still smells like death, dung

Cool science images:

The Why Files
http://whyfiles.news.wisc.edu/index.html

NSF sponsors an excellent weekly on-line magazine that addresses current science questions in the news. Recent articles include life on Mars and how tropical storms form. Available files in this site include Cloning, Migration, Climatology, Neutrinos, and Electric Cars.

R	GL	TCK	RR	STS	IL	RTD
**	8–12	*	*	*	*	

INTEGRATING SCIENCE AND OTHER CURRICULAR AREAS

EE-Link: Environmental Education Resources on the Internet
http://nceet.snre.umich.edu/

A wide variety of environmental education resources are available at this site. It includes separate classroom resources sections for teachers and students. Curriculum guides, lessons activities, and lists of links are all available.

R	GL	TCK	RR	STS	IL	RTD
*	8–10	*	*	*	*	

Reading the Skies
http://curry.edschool.Virginia.EDU/~tgt3e/skies/

Provides a framework for interdisciplinary instruction and accompanying lesson plans on astronomy and literature. The topic index includes:

- Introduction—Van Gogh, Walt Whitman; How do humans use the stars?
- Time—Hootie and the Blowfish, Shakespeare, archaeoastronomy
- Constellations—oral traditions; astronomy: fact and fiction
- The Moon—tidal charts, "Two Leading Lights," the Dave Matthews Band
- Our Solar System—*The Martian Chronicles,* "Fire and Ice"
- Astronomers—Indigo Girls, historical links, and the *Spoon River Anthology*
- Stars and Galaxies—Robert Frost and cosmology
- Space Exploration and Colonization—Toad, Bradbury, colony design
- Epilogue

R	GL	TCK	RR	STS	IL	RTD
*	6–12	*	*	*		

Reprinted courtesy of Smithsonian Office of Education.

SOE Home Page
http://educate.si.edu/

Smithsonian Education provides on-line lesson plans from its quarterly magazine, Smithsonian in Your Classroom, integrating science and other curriculum areas. To find these plans, click on recent issues of Smithsonian in Your Classroom. More lesson plans from back issues are also available at this site. There are six interdisciplinary marine science lesson plans from the Smithsonian Ocean Planet exhibition. For more than 500 educational materials from the museum collection, click on Teachers Resources.

R	GL	TCK	RR	STS	IL	RTD
**	6–12	*	*	*	*	*

Reprinted with permission of the Center for Adolescent Studies.

Teacher Talk Forum
http://education.indiana.edu/cas/ttforum/ttforum.html

The Center for Adolescent Studies at the Indiana University School of Education provides a collection of electronic lesson plans for science and health. Menu headings available at this site are: News, Lesson Plans, Professional Development Resources, Teacher References, Cyber Schools, Internet Fieldtrips, Museums, Technology in the Classroom, and References for Kids.

R	GL	TCK	RR	STS	IL	RTD
**	10–12	*	*	*	*	

CHAPTER SUMMARY

This chapter has provided you with many sites that will enable you to implement the National Science Education Standards. The sites identified in this chapter foster deeper understanding of science in its diverse domains. Just a click with the mouse at the sites provided in this chapter allows you to communicate with communities of scientists, science education researchers, teachers, and students. Science teachers and their students can actually have distant mentors answering their questions.

Reference

National Research Council (1996). *National Science Education Standards.*
    Washington, DC: National Academy Press.

4

SCIENCE CURRICULAR FRAMEWORKS

- Scientific Inquiry and the Nature of Science
- Teaching for Conceptual Change
- Assessment
- Concept Mapping
- Journal Writing in the Classroom
- Girls and Science
- Multicultural Science Education
- Science, Technology, and Society (STS)
- Informal Learning
- Professional Organizations

The National Science Standards also include standards for science teaching, standards for professional development, standards for assessment in science education, standards for science education programs, and standards for science education systems (National Research Council, 1996, pp. 3–8). Hence, this book has included not only the Internet sites that pertain to the science content standards but also sites that will lead to the understanding of major topics and issues in science education.

Directory of Science Education Websites
http://www-sul.stanford.edu/depts/swain/nsflibnews/dosew.html

This site provides a directory of associations, Web search engines, education databases, Web directories for science education sources, Web directories with science categories, sites for cool science links and current events in science education.

Index
http://academic.wsc.edu/education/sweetland_r/ccmppp

Dr. Robert Sweetland interprets Jazlin V. Ebenezer's and Sylvia Connor's Common Knowledge Construction Model for teaching science in this site.

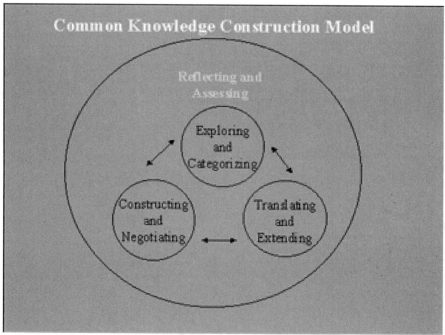

Adapted from Learning to Teach Science: A Model for the 21st Century, by Ebenezer and Connor, 1998, page 97.

Reprinted with permission of Anthony W. Lorbach, Illinois State University.

The Learning Cycle as a Tool for Planning Science Instruction
www.coe.ilstu.edu/scienceed/lorsbach/257lrcy.htm

Anthony W. Lorsbach offers a five-part learning cycle in this site. It is an established planning method in science education and consistent with contemporary theories about how individuals learn. It is easy to learn and useful in creating opportunities to learn science.

The 5 E Learning Cycle Model
www.mwsu.edu/~educ/coe/inquire/inquiry.htm

Connections are facilitated between what students know and can do.

Learning Cycle Lesson Plans
www.bamaed.ua.edu/~amays/learning_cycle_lesson_plans.htm

This site provides samples of lesson plans based on the learning cycle.

Learning Cycle Instructional Model
mvhs1.mbhs.edu/mvhsproj/learningcycle/lc.htm

This site describes the connection between the learning cycle and constructivism.

Philosophy—Learning Cycles and Styles
www.aenc.org/ABOUT/Philosophy-Learning.html

The learning cycle and learning styles are connected in this site. It helps a teacher quickly perceive that no two students learn in exactly the same ways at identical speeds.

The Inquiry Page
http://www.inquiry.vivc.edu

This site provides a visual diagram of the steps in the learning cycle, which involves evaluating, elaborating, explaining, exploring and engaging. The Inquiry Page is more than a Web site. It's a dynamic virtual community where inquiry-based education can be discussed, resources and experiences shared, and innovative approaches explored in a collaborative environment.

The Science Learning Cycle
www.holland.k12.mi.us/curriculum/sci.cycle.html

This site illustrates how the learning cycle can be used for activating prior knowledge and invites students to share their thinking.

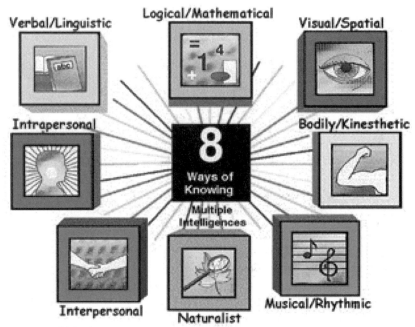

Source: www.multi-intel.com.

Exploring Multiple Intelligences: New Dimensions of Learning
http://www.multi-intell.com/

Exploring Multiple Intelligences is sponsored by New Dimensions of Learning. This site answers the questions: What is multiple intelligence? Where is it being implemented? What resources are available? What training opportunities exist? Lesson ideas are provided.

An Explanation of Learning Styles and Multiple Intelligence (MI)
http://www.ldpride.net/learningstyles.MI.htm

Find out what learning styles are all about and assess your own learning style/MI in this site.

Multiple Intelligence Theory: Principles
http://www.harding.edu/~cbr/midemo/prin.html

Resources in teaching and introduction to multiple intelligence theory and principles are provided in this site.

Multiple Intelligences: Theory and Practice in the K–12 Classroom
http://eric.indiana.edu/www/indexdb.html

This site provides MI bibliography of Web and paper-based resources.

The Toolroom: Resource: Howard Gardner: Theory of Multiple Intelligences
http://www.newhorizons.org/trm_gardner.html

This site provides resources to explore Gardner's Theory of Multiple Intelligences, which suggests that our culture, and school systems that reflect our culture, teach, test, reinforce and reward primarily two kinds of intelligence: verbal/linguistic and logical/mathematical.

Multiple Intelligence Sound Unit
http://www.ed.mtu.edu/esmis/id71.htm

This site provides a unit on sound for Grade 6. The unit illustrates each of the multiple intelligences.

Source: The University of Georgia College of Education. Copyright ©1996 Shawn Glynn

Teaching with Analogies
http://www.coe.uga.edu/edpsych/faculty/glynn/twa.html

This Web site highlights a new, research-based method for teaching science concepts in the schools. This method uses analogies to help children form initial mental models of key science concepts.

SCIENTIFIC INQUIRY AND THE NATURE OF SCIENCE

Chapter 1: The Nature of Science
http://www.project2061.org/tools/sfaaol/chap1.htm

This site presents *Science for All Americans,* a book about science literacy, by Project 2061—American Association for the Advancement of Science. It is important reading for all science teachers and science teacher educators.

Chapter 2: Inquiry in the National Science Education Standards
http://www.nap.edu/html/inquiry_addendum/ch2.html

Chapter 2 of the National Science Education Standards is presented in this site. Inquiry in the National Standards encompasses not only an ability to engage in inquiry but an understanding of inquiry and of how inquiry results in scientific knowledge.

Scientific Inquiry and NOS
http://www.orst.edu/dept/csfa/scinat.html

This site provides an understanding of scientific inquiry. Scientific inquiry refers to the various processes and strategies that scientists employ in an attempt to answer questions of interest. There is not a single set of steps that scientists follow in all investigations.

The Nature of Scientific Inquiry
http://www.inform.umd.edu/EdRes/Colleges/ARHU/Depts/Philosophy/homepage/faculty/LDarden/sciing/

Cases of famous scientists who did good work but also made honest mistakes. A historian and philosopher of science describes several such scientists.

Scientific Inquiry
http://www.bios.niu.edu/sims/bios103/Lecture2

This site provides a table of contents with scientific inquiry standards of evidence.

Oregon Common Curriculum Goals for Scientific Inquiry
http://www.orst.edu/Dept/sci_mth_education/course/ORCurrGoals.html

This site outlines Oregon's Common Curriculum Goals for Scientific Inquiry. HISTORY AND NATURE OF SCIENCE portrays science as a human endeavor, characterizes the nature of scientific knowledge, and describes the history of science as it relates to and clarifies scientific inquiries.

BOL Ch. 1—The Nature of Science
http://www.project2061.org/tools/benchol/ch1/ch1.htm

The Nature of Science characterizes the scientific world view and scientific inquiry. Educational goals in terms of the scientific world view and scientific inquiry are provided in this site for Kindergarten through Grade 2, Grades 3 through 5, Grades 6 through 8, and Grades 9 through 12.

The State of Science Education: Subject Matter Without Context
http://www.chem.vt.edu/confchem/1998/lederman/lederman.html

Norman G. Lederman contributed the keynote paper to *Switching Students on to Science*, the Fall 1998 On-Line Conference on Chemistry Education and Research. It is reproduced in full at this site.

Science and the Scientific Method
http://www.srikant.org/core/node2.html

Science and the scientific method are described in this site.

Draft of the Scientific Inquiry Scoring Guide
http://www.col-ed.org/smcnws/scientific.html

This site presents a draft of the scientific inquiry scoring guide, which includes correctly applying concepts, information, theories, and research specific to the domain of inquiry. Terminology, notations, and formulas from the domain of inquiry are precisely used.

Scientific Method Template	
GOAL	identify environmental causes of cancer
MODEL	power plants cause cancer
DATA (1st set)	higher cancer rates near power plants
DATA (2nd set)	higher cancer rates at proposed sites
EVALUATION	the model is inconsistent with data set 2
REVISION	reject the model and choose an alternative

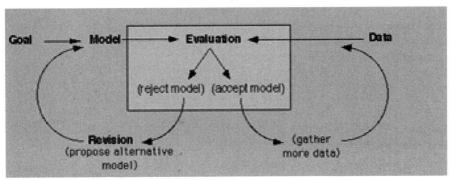

Source: www.common-nonsense.com.

A Template for Scientific Inquiry
http://www.common-nonsense.com/Scientific_Method/Scientific.method/Text.cfm

A site which points out an underlying structure with five basic elements: goals, models, data, evaluation, and revision, despite the complexities of scientific method. Examples illustrate the five elements.

ScienceNetLinks: Nature of Science—Lessons: 3–5 Lessons
http://www.sciencenetlinks.com/curriculum/natsci/lessons_3-5.html

Lesson plans for Grades 3–5 illustrate the nature of science. Lessons are based on the scientific world view, scientific inquiry, images of science, and the scientific enterprise. Related weekly science is updated.

ScienceNetLinks: Nature of Science—Lessons: 9–12 Lessons
http://www.sciencenetlinks.com/curriculum/natsci/lessons_9-12.html

Nature of Science—Lessons are available for Grades 9–12 in this site. Cracking the genetic code is an example. Weekly updates are provided.

National Standards 5–12
http://lifesci3.arc.nasa.gov/SpaceSettlement/teacher/standards

This site provides lesson plans for Grades 5–8 on space settlement based on National Science Standards conceptions of science as inquiry.

Observations
http://scienceathome.mwsi.net/observations.htm

This site emphasizes observations in scientific inquiry. Scientific inquiry begins by making observations about things in nature. Next, the scientist asks questions about something of interest. Finally, scientists conduct investigations to find the answers to their questions.

TEACHING FOR CONCEPTUAL CHANGE

Teaching for Conceptual Change
http://www.exploratorium.edu/IFI/resources/workshops/
teachingforconcept.html

Teaching for conceptual change involves confronting children's experience, according to Bruce Watson and Richard Kopnicek (*Phi Delta Kappan* May 1990, pp. 680–684).

Teaching With Analogies
http://www.coe.uga.edu/edpsych/faculty/glynn/twa.html

This Web site highlights a new, research-based method for teaching science concepts in the schools. This method uses analogies to help children form initial mental models of key science concepts.

Students' Alternate Conceptions

Students' Alternate Conceptions
phys.udallas.edu/C3P/altconcp.html

Students' alternate conceptions are listed for various topics in introductory physics. These conceptions can be incorporated into learning strategies.

Teaching Strategies Dealing With Students' Alternate Conceptions
www.fed.cuhk.edu.hk/~johnson/misconceptions/ce/misonceptions/
instructional/instructional.htm

Teaching strategies for dealing with students' alternative conceptions in biology are available in this site.

ASSESSMENT

Martha's Alternative Assessment in Science List
http://www.crpc.rice.edu/CRPC/GT/mborrow/Lessons/assessls.html

Martha Phelps-Borrowman's compilation of various sites on alternative assessment in science is available in this site.

Reprinted with permission of the Miami Museum of Science, Inc.

Miami Museum of Science—Alternative Assessment
http://www.miamisci.org/ph/

The paradigm shift from the traditional teacher-directed classroom to a more active learning, student-based classroom has created the need for educators to re-evaluate the ways they have previously assessed. Performance assessment is based on teacher observations of a student's performance or samples of various projects done by the student.

Alternative Assessment
http://www.emtech.net/Alternative_Assessment.html

Links and resources on alternative or performance assessment are available in this site.

Alternative Strategies for Science Teaching and Assessment
http://science.uniserve.edu.au/school/support/strategy.html

This site provides alternative strategies for science teaching and assessment, which includes virtual field trips, case studies, debates, problem-based learning, role play, mysteries, posters and portfolios, WebQuests and treasure hunts, cyber guides, mini-conferences, plays, concept maps, and court cases.

Elementary Science: Ideas for Assessment
http://www.sasked.gov.sk.ca/docs/elemsci/ideass.html

Assessment ideas for the elementary science classroom in this site include conferences, interviews, contracts, portfolios, and conferencing with groups as they work, recording responses on an anecdotal/observational grid.

Authentic Assessments
http://www.ncrel.org/sdrs/areas/issues/educatrs/leadrshp/le4ass.htm

This site describes what is meant by authentic assessment. Authentic assessment involves procedures that have meaning beyond the assessment process, are in-depth, and often require performance by the student that demonstrates deeper understanding and skills.

Assessment Resources
http://www.bridge-rayn.org/teacher.html

This site presents a well-collected list of alternative assessments that matches with the national standards.

Assessment
http://www.col-ed.org/smcnws/assessment.html

This site is a compilation of international, national, state and district collections of assessment tasks. Alternative assessment techniques are taken from ERIC: An introductory bibliography.

Exemplars: Standards-Based Performance Assessment and Instruction
http://www.exemplars.com/science_k-8_product.html

Performance assessment investigations are provided in this site for Grades K–8 that meet national science standards.

Implementing Curriculum, Instruction, and Assessment Standards for Science Education
http://www.ncrel.org/sdrs/areas/issues/content/cntareas/science/sc300.htm

The American Association for the Advancement of Science and the National Research Council have proposed important new standards on critical issues in science education, which include implementing curriculum, instruction, and assessment for science education.

Middle Level Science: Assessment and Evaluation
http://www.sasked.gov.sk.ca/docs/midlsci/asevmsc.html

This site asks the question: Why Consider Assessment and Evaluation? Much research in education around the world is currently focusing on assessment and evaluation.

Performance Assessment
http://www.ed.gov/pubs/OR/ConsumerGuides/perfasse.html

This site explores the meaning of performance assessment. Performance assessment, also known as alternative or authentic assessment, is a form of testing that requires students to perform a task rather than select an answer from a ready-made list.

Science Process Assessments for Elementary and Middle School Students
http://users.penn.com/~ksmith/s&w.html

This site details science process assessments for elementary and middle school students, which are easy-to-administer paper/pencil tests designed to measure the 13 science process skills.

ENC Online
http://www.enc.org/

This site is the best selection of K–12 mathematics and science curriculum resources on the Internet, and includes assessment.

CONCEPT MAPPING

Concept Mapping
http://www.graphic.org/concept.html

This site provides a description of concept mapping for exploring knowledge and gathering and sharing information.

Concept Mapping
www.mdk12.org/practices/good_instruction/projectbetter/science/s-1-2.htm

This site presents the use of concept mapping from topics dealing with the cartography of cognition to science curriculum development to conceptual change.

Problem Solving
http://www.cotf.edu/ete/pbl2.html

This site describes concept mapping as a good way to organize information about a problem or subject. Construction of concept maps helps to pull together information we already know about a subject and understand how new information is related.

The Graphic Organizer
http://www.graphic.org/

The Graphic Organizer is the premier Web site for information about graphic organizers, concept maps, and visual tools.

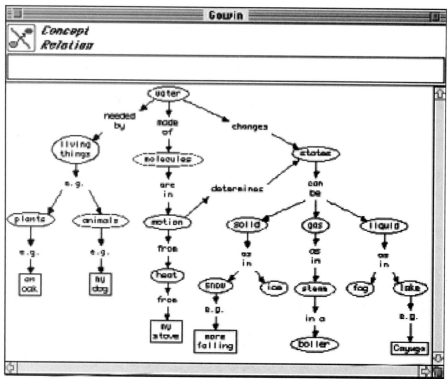

Source: Novak and Gowin, 1984.

Learning Skills Program—Concept Mapping
http://www.coun.uvic.ca/learn/program/hndouts/map_ho.html

This site introduces concept mapping as a tool for assisting and enhancing many of the types of thinking and learning that we are required to do at college.

An Introduction to Concept Mapping for Planning and Evaluation
http://trochim.human.cornell.edu/research/epp1/epp1.htm

This site provides an introduction to concept mapping for planning and evaluation.

Concept Mapping: Soft Science or Hard Art?
http://trochim.human.cornell.edu/research/epp2/epp2.htm

The author asks the question whether concept mapping is soft science or hard art?

Concept Mapping and Curriculum Design
http://www.utc.edu/Teaching-Resource-Center/concepts.html

This site links concept mapping and curriculum design. It asks the question: What is a concept map? It shows concept mapping and curriculum design steps in making a concept map. There is a discussion on constructivism. There are references to other reading on the Internet dealing with concept maps.

WebMap: Concept Mapping on the Web
http://ksi.cpsc.ucalgary.ca/articles/WWW/WWW4WM/WWW4WM.html

Knowledge Science Institute, University of Calgary, Alberta, Canada shows how to do concept maps on the Web.

Year 1 and 2: Cooperative Learning
http://idea.uml.edu/assessment/vaughn1.html
http://idea.uml.edu/assessment/vaughn2.html

These sites describe concept mapping and cooperative learning. They also provide activities for alternative assessments in K–12 education.

Biology Instructional Philosophy: Concept Mapping
http://www.biologylessons.sdsu.edu/philosophy/conceptmap.html

This site contains a bibliography of articles dealing with concept mapping, some of which are specifically biology-oriented.

JOURNAL WRITING IN THE CLASSROOM

Journal Writing in the Classroom
http://k-6educators.about.com/library/weekly/aa100100a.htm

This site provides ideas, tips, and story starters for journal writing in the classroom.

Education World
http://www.education-world.com/a_curr/curr144.shtml

This site indicates many ways teachers can use journal writing to meet specific goals. Some teachers monitor journal writing and work on polishing skills.

GIRLS AND SCIENCE

Girls and Science
http://www.edtech.wednet.edu/equity/research/54.html

Equity Education On Line presents Girls and Science, a quarterly newsletter that includes news, books, resources, and hands-on science experiments for girls of all ages interested in science.

Why girls turn their backs on a science education
http://www.lboro.ac.uk/orgs/opp2000/chap2.htm

The question, "Why do girls turn their backs on a science education?" is answered in this site. Barriers in the early school years, secondary school level, and at the tertiary level are explored.

Internet for Girls: World Wide Web Resource List
http://www.sdsc.edu/~woodka/resources.html

Here you will find resources in mathematics and science, parent resources, teacher resources, and links to sites created especially for women and girls.

ENC: How Things Work: Helping Girls Explore Technology
http://www.enc.org/topics/equity/articles/document.shtm1321_bi

The ENC site provides topics, equity, and journal articles for girls in science. Timely ideas and information, with daily updates, are also presented. Complete information about thousands of teaching materials for K–12 math and science are available in this site.

Research in Math/Science Education for Girls
http://www.cs.utexas.edu/users/cline/ear/research.html

This site presents research reports, AAUW research initiatives, and nine steps to achieving gender equity in science classrooms, plus links to other sites. Also, the AAUW Selected Bibliography on Gender Equity is available.

NC Museum of Natural Sciences—Education: Girls in Science
http://www.naturalsciences.org/education/girlsci.html

The Girls in Science Statewide Project encourages girls who are interested in science. Girls in Science programs provide hands-on activities with living things in a safe atmosphere where a girl's natural scientific curiosity can flourish.

Expect the Best from a Girl
http://www.academic.org/

This site encourages girls to reach their full potential, especially in the spheres of science and math.

Gender Issues in Science Education
http://www.msu.edu/user/brownme1

Gender issues in science education are discussed by Jennifer Brown, Melissa Brown, Nicole Nelson, & David Piotrowski. Related links and resources: Women in Science, National Women's History Project, Women of NASA, Association for Women in Science.

Girls and Women in Science
http://www.beloit.edu/~gwsci

The question, "What is GWS?" is answered in this site. It also discusses gender issues in science and math, provides Web resources, and contact information for a project for sixth-grade girls, their teachers, and parents.

CAMEL—Women—Education
http://camel.math.ca/Women/EDU/Education.html

How do we make sure that girls receive an equitable education in mathematics? And what exactly does "equitable" mean, as distinct from "equal"?

MULTICULTURAL SCIENCE EDUCATION

Science: Multicultural Education Resources
http://nasc.uwyo.edu/wcms/Science/Resources/MulticulLinks.htm

This site provides descriptions of and links to the following Web sites:

- Achieving Gender Equity in Science Classrooms
- Making Schools Work for Every Child
- Other Web Sites on Women and Science
- The Consortium for Equity in Standards and Testing
- The Faces of Science: African Americans in the Sciences
- 4,000 Years of Women in Science

Multicultural Science Education
www.upei.ca/~xliu/multi-culture/home.htm

Cultural contributions are presented in this site. Science subjects are astronomy, biology, chemistry, engineering, medicine, and physics. Table of contents, ethnic scientists, annotated bibliography, links to related sites, comments and suggestions are included in this site.

BI97Life\BI97Temp\BI97Temp
www.woodrow.org/teachers/bi/1997/multicul/

A multicultural approach to teaching a science lesson is the main objective of this site. A brief summary is included on what multicultural science education is and why it is important that we teach it. The site models a lesson on African American scientist Ernest Just's experiment on parthenogenesis.

Multicultural Science Lessons and Resources
http://www.cloudnet.com/~edrbsass/edmulticult.htm#science

This site lists descriptions of and links to multicultural science lesson plans for a variety of grade levels. Links include:

- Alaska Native Knowledge Network
- Multicolor, Multicultural Lesson on Elements, Mixtures, and Compounds
- Houses Around the World
- Myths, Legends, and Moon Phases
- An Appreciation of the World's Ever-Shrinking Rain Forests
- Finding Out About Herbs in Latin America
- Why Is There Pollution in Mexico City?
- African American Scientists

SCIENCE, TECHNOLOGY AND SOCIETY

Science, Technology and Society
www.nde.state.ne.us/SS/sts.html

Nebraska teachers offer information, resources, and activities pertaining to the theme of *Science, Technology and Society*.

Integrating Science and Technology in the Science Classroom
www.tamu-commerce.edu/coe/shed/espinoza/s/ellis-b-657.html

Lesson plans integrating science and technology are presented in this site—A MUST for classroom science teachers!

Lesson Plans—Bridges
school.discovery.com/lessonplans/programs/bridges/

Lesson plans on building bridges show the relationships among science, technology, and society.

INFORMAL LEARNING

Science Learning Network
Funding Provided by Unisys & The National Science Foundation

Source: The Science Learning Network.

Science Learning Network
http://sln.org/info/index.html

The Science Learning Network is a partnership among six science museums and Unisys Corporation that integrates educational resources offered by these science/technology centers with the power of telecomputing to provide new support for teacher development and science learning.

The Exploratorium—The museum of science, art, and human perception
http://www.exploratorium.edu/

This site presents interactive on-line exhibits and exhibitions, hands-on activities, Webcasts, and more from a museum in San Francisco.

Reprinted with permission of NSTA.

PROFESSIONAL ORGANIZATIONS

NSTA
http://www.nsta.org/

This site provides information about the National Science Teachers Association (NSTA), the largest organization in the world committed to promoting excellence and innovation in science teaching and learning for all. It includes links to state, national, and international science education organizations; an on-line catalog of publications; and two chat rooms to foster interaction and ongoing conversations about science education.

NSTA's current membership is more than 53,000.This includes science teachers, science supervisors, administrators, scientists, business and industry representatives, and others involved in science education.

NSTA addresses subjects of critical interest to science educators. The Association publishes five journals, a newspaper, many books, a new children's magazine called Dragonfly, and many other publications. NSTA conducts national and regional conventions that attract more than 30,000 attendees annually.

NSTA provides many programs and services for science educators including awards, professional development workshops, and educational tours. NSTA offers professional certification for science teachers in eight teaching levels and discipline area categories.

NSTA's newest and largest initiative to date, Building a Presence for Science, seeks to improve science education and align science teaching to the National Science Education Standards nationwide. The Exxon Education Foundation has funded the initial effort to bring the program to 10 states and the District of Columbia.

The Association serves as an advocate for science educators by keeping its members and the general public informed about national issues and trends in science education. NSTA disseminates results from nationwide surveys and reports and offers testimony to Congress on science education-related legislation and other issues. The organization has position statements on issues such as teacher preparation, laboratory science, the use of animals in the classroom, laboratory safety, and elementary and middle-level science.

NSTA is involved in cooperative working relationships with numerous educational organizations, government agencies, and private industries on a variety of projects.

NSTA Press Release Archive
http://www.nsta.org/pressroom

This site provides information as to how NSTA assists teachers to implement the National Science Education Standards in their classrooms. The Framework for High School Science Education shows how the content standards can be sequenced and integrated over four years of high school.

NSTA's Scope, Sequence and Coordination Project
http://dev.nsta.org/ssc

Scope, Sequence and Coordination is a NSTA project funded by the National Science Foundation. The project focuses on creating science programs at the secondary level based on the National Science Education Standards. This Web site offers several micro-units that are composed of labs, readings and assessments for teachers and students.

Association for the Education of Teachers in Science
http://aets.chem.pitt.edu

This site provides information about the Association for the Education of Teachers in Science. It promotes leadership and provides support for those involved in the professional development of teachers. This includes teachers who:

- Teach science education courses for prospective teachers
- Provide in-service programs for elementary, middle level, or secondary teachers of science
- Supervise, advise, or coordinate teachers in science
- Develop new approaches or materials for science teacher education
- Conduct action research
- Supervise graduate students in science education
- Develop electronic media for use in science education

AMERICAN ASSOCIATION FOR THE ADVANCEMENT OF SCIENCE

Source: American Association for the Advancement of Science.

The American Association for the Advancement of Science
http://www.aaas.org/

This site provides information about the American Association for Advancement of Science (AAAS, pronounced "Triple-A-S"), a nonprofit professional society dedicated to the advancement of scientific and technological excellence across all disciplines and to the public's understanding of science and technology. AAAS is among the oldest societies in America, having been founded in Philadelphia in 1848. Many of today's most prestigious and influential scientific societies have their historical origins in AAAS. For example, groups such as the American Chemical Society (1886), the American Anthropological Association (1902), and the Botanical Society of America (1906) all grew out of informal gatherings at AAAS annual meetings or from established AAAS sections.

According to AAAS's constitution, its mission is to:

■ Further the work of scientists
■ Facilitate cooperation among them

- Foster scientific freedom and responsibility
- Improve the effectiveness of science in the promotion of human welfare
- Advance education in science
- Increase the public's understanding and appreciation of the promise of scientific methods in human progress

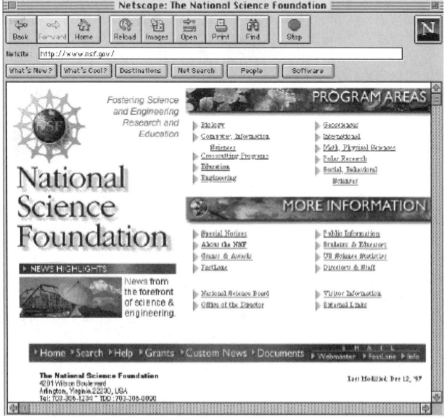

Source: National Science Foundation.

National Science Foundation
http://www.nsf.gov/

This site provides information about the National Science Foundation. It is an independent U.S. government agency responsible for promoting science and engineering through programs that invest over $3.3 billion per year in almost 20,000 research and education projects in science and engineering.

Source: NASA

NASA Homepage
http://www.nasa.gov/

This is the homepage of NASA. NASA is committed to disseminating aeronautics and space research and provides education resources on the following strategic enterprises:

- Aeronautics
- Human Exploration and Development of Space
- Mission to Planet Earth
- Space Science

References

National Research Council (1996). *National Science Education Standards.* Washington, DC: National Academy Press.

Watson, B., & Kopnicek, R. (1990, May). Teaching for conceptual change: Confronting children's experience. *Phi Delta Kappan,* pp. 680–684.